Partners

In collaboration with:

Freie Universität Berlin
Sciences Po Paris
Université Libre de Bruxelles
ESC Dijon, Burgundy School of Business
University of Bergamo

With the financial support of:

European Union
ESCEM
Ernst & Young Wirtschaftsprüfungsgesellschaft GmbH
Capgemini Italy
Sanofi-Aventis Italy
Sogeti

We thank the following professors for having participated in the Selection Committee: Marek Hudon (Université Libre de Bruxelles), Arvind Ashta (ESC Dijon), Adalbert Winkler (Frankfurt School of Finance and Management), Jean-Michel Servet (Graduate Institute of International and Development Studies Geneva), Manfred Nitsch (Freie Universität Berlin), Christina Wildenauer (TU Berlin), Ana Marr (Greenwich University), Laura Vigano (University of Bergamo), Baptiste Venet (University of Dauphine), Stephan Klasen / Ahmad Nawaz (University of Goettingen) and Andreas Woudenberg (INHolland University of applied Science The Hague).

UNIVERSITY MEETS MICROFINANCE

edited by PlaNet Finance Deutschland e.V.

ISSN 2190-2291

The "University Meets Microfinance" programme (UMM) presents its third "UMM Award":

Each year, the UMM Awards honour outstanding theses on microfinance and give recognition to the work of young researchers. The UMM Award winners are selected by a committee of professors and microfinance practitioners, to recognise theses presenting innovative research topics and approaches.
Microfinance has gained scale and recognition over the last decade. Today, Microfinance Institutions reach approximately 150 million low-income people who were previously excluded from formal banking systems, with financial services which include credit, savings, insurance and money transfer. This rapid expansion has also come with increasing challenges.
Research on microfinance provides new insights into these challenges and can foster innovation in the sector.
In 2009, 720 practitioners, students and professors from 14 universities of the European Union participated in UMM. The programme is co-financed by the European Union and was initiated by PlaNet Finance and Freie Universität Berlin with the aim of strengthening the cooperation between European universities and microfinance practitioners. In addition to promoting research publications, UMM offers microfinance seminars in partnership with European universities, mentorship and field research scholarships for Bachelor, Master and PhD students, and organises regular workshops with UMM participants.

More information can be found at
www.universitymeetsmicrofinance.eu and www.planetfinance.org

Volumes

1 *Pim Engels*
Mission Drift in Microfinance
The Influence of Institutional and Country Risk Indicators on the Trade-Off between the Financial and Social Performance of Microfinance Institutions
ISBN 978-3-8382-0123-8

2 *Thilo Klein*
Microfinance 2.0
Group Formation and Repayment Performance in Online Lending Platforms During the US Credit Crunch
ISBN 978-3-8382-0118-4

3 *Saikumar C. Bharamappanavara*
The Performance Of Microcredit Organisations
A Comparative Perspective
ISBN 978-3-8382-0121-4

Saikumar C. Bharamappanavara

THE PERFORMANCE OF MICROCREDIT ORGANISATIONS

A Comparative Perspective

ibidem-Verlag
Stuttgart

Bibliografische Information der Deutschen Nationalbibliothek
Die Deutsche Nationalbibliothek verzeichnet diese Publikation in der Deutschen Nationalbibliografie; detaillierte bibliografische Daten sind im Internet über http://dnb.d-nb.de abrufbar.

Bibliographic information published by the Deutsche Nationalbibliothek
Die Deutsche Nationalbibliothek lists this publication in the Deutsche Nationalbibliografie; detailed bibliographic data are available in the Internet at http://dnb.d-nb.de.

Gedruckt auf alterungsbeständigem, säurefreien Papier
Printed on acid-free paper

ISSN: 2190-2291

ISBN-13: 978-3-8382-0121-4

Printed in Germany

Foreword

Mr Saikumar C. Bharamappanavara completed his graduation studies in Agriculture from the University of Agricultural Sciences, Bangalore, and received his Masters in Agricultural Economics from the University of Agricultural Sciences, Dharwad, India. He later secured a Masters in International Masters Rural Development (IMRD) through the EU-Erasmus Mundus scholarship from the University of Ghent and Humboldt University of Berlin. The IMRD conferred on him the "great distinction" award for his excellent academic performance. The "University Meets Microfinance (UMM) Award 2009" of the Europe Union was conferred for his "best thesis" and outstanding research work on microfinance, enunciated in this publication and provided in brief below. With his continued research interest in the microfinance field, he is presently doing his PhD with DAAD fellowship at Humboldt University of Berlin in a project funded by the German Federal Ministry of Research and Education on "Climate and Energy in a Complex Transition Process towards Sustainable Hyderabad Mitigation and Adaptation Strategies by Changing Institutions, Governance Structures, Lifestyles and Consumption Pattern- Sustainable Hyderabad (India)".

Self-Help Group (SHG) microcredit is emerging as a springboard of developmental finance for Income Generating Activities (IGAs) in rural areas of India, serving the cause of the landless, small, and marginal households. SHG peer pressure is the primary driver of impressive repayment performance. Present field research in India reveals that homogeneity of SHG members and freedom of participation in SHG deliberations are primarily responsible for strengthening collective action. Specifically, the savings and loan per capita, satisfactory performance of organisation, awareness of SHG linkage, the family size, and age-induced responsibility were found to strongly influence the economic performance of SHGs. These are the key drivers of sustainability of SHGs for their welfare. Using logical empirical evidence, this book amply demonstrates the emergence of prime factors determining the performance of SHGs in India by examining their organisational behaviour and recommends appropriate policies for social cloning.

Dr V R Kiresur
Senior Scientist (Economics)
International Crops Research Institute for the Semi-Arid Tropics (ICRISAT)

Editorial

Group-based banking has become the primary mode of microfinance in India. Village peer-groups of 10 to 20 members organise savings and repayment and form the basic collective mechanism by which per unit cost and risks of rating can be dramatically reduced. In rural India, though all Self-Help Groups (SHGs) are financed by banks, different "actors" like the government, NGOs, and banks themselves organise and incentivise the formation of these groups. Systematic differences exist in the factors like the amount of capacity-building given, the relative cost of access to credit, the process of group formation, and the respective homogeneity among the members – these "differences" constitute the point of departure for Saikumar C. Bharamappanavara's comparative analysis. In his empirical study in Karnataka, India, he analyses how performance of three different SHG-models varies with these different actors involved.

In his results, he differentiates particular classes of variables, institutional factors, as well as social and economic factors that affect the performance of the SHGs. In his sample, Self-Help Groups initiated by banks perform relatively better than those formed by NGOs and government organisations. This result underpins the thesis that banks – through whom providing credit is often comparatively costly – have a more professional attitude towards credit-giving and are likely to provide the most effective form of capacity-building to group members. This interpretation gains additional importance through his finding that a credit acquisition at relatively higher cost seems to have a disciplinant effect on the overall performance of the analysed Self-Help Groups. Saikumar C. Bharamappanavara's analysis does not stop here. Following the literature on group behaviour and collective-action theory, he investigates the roles of member-participation and the members` perceptions of trust and transparency on the social performance of group-based banking. His study impressively confirms the importance of these factors. With these results, Saikumar C. Bharamappanavara's work is equally relevant for decision makers and researchers in the areas of development studies and microfinance.

Prof. Dr. Markus Hanisch
Professor of Cooperatives Sciences,
Humboldt University of Berlin

Acknowledgement

It is my pleasure to express and share my feelings with the following people, without whom I may not have achieved this goal.

I express my profound and deepest gratitude to my Advisor, Prof Dr Markus Hanisch, Head of the Division of Cooperative Sciences, for his continuous support, encouragement, and patient instructions, which always boosted my confidence. I humbly thank him for his illuminating guidance, perceptual interest, precious suggestions, and ever helping mind at every step throughout the period of study.

I am strongly beholden to all respondents of the study who have cordially responded to my survey questionnaire.

I would like to thank the European Union for providing an opportunity to study the IMRD Programme with financial and logistic support. I am grateful to all the professors, IMRD secretariat, and Prof Dr Guido Van Huylenbroeck for their invaluable support throughout the study period. I extend my regards to all the coordinators and staff members of Gent University, Humboldt University, and the University of Pisa for making this programme a memorable one.

My special thanks to Jens Rommel, Pradeep Kumar N.O., Jeroen Buysse, and Dr Lalith Achoth for their keen interest, encouragement, and valuable suggestions during the course of my study.

I am immensely grateful to Santhosh, Girish, Naveen, Dr Vageesh, Dr Pradeep and Jr. Pradeep, Mallikarjun, Prasanna B.K. and Sunya, Ashoka, Mahesh for their kind help and strong support during my data collection.

I also extend my thanks to Prof Dr V.R. Kiresur, Prof Dr M.G. Chandrakanth, and Prof Dr S.M. Mundinamani and to all other professors in the Department of Agricultural Economics from UAS (Dharwad) and UAS (Bangalore).

It is with great pride and joy that I extend my heartiest thanks to my ever-encouraging friends Akarsha, Monish, Manjunath, Tejaswi, Gayathri, Nithya, Laxmi, Rashmi, Vishal, Rajeshwari, Poornima, Anu, Anoop, Deepesh, Jayasimha, Surya, and Ananth for their immense support and encouragement. I can not skip my special thanks to all other IMRD friends, juniors, and seniors for being with me all the time in last two years and for giving me the remarkable memories to carry in life.

It is a great pleasure to acknowledge the help extended by NABARD, District Statistical Office, Women and Child Development Department (GOK), officials of the Department of Agriculture (Davanagere Dist.), and ICDO-NGO officials for providing the necessary information required during the course of the field work.

I owe a lot to all my Under Graduate, Post Graduate friends, juniors, and seniors, Bhadravathi and family friends, who are my precious assets in life. I convey my wholehearted thanks to Shashikumar, Dr Naveenkumar Shetty, Gireeshayya, near and dear ones, and all the members in the Bharamappanavara and Sannalingklara families.

I am at a loss of words to express my sincere feelings, affectionate and heartfelt thanks to my parents Smt. Channamma and Sri. Cheelurappa B., dearest brothers Dr Gangadhar, Manjunath, sister Prema and to my Uncle Hanumanthappa B. for their never-ending support, affection, love, and sacrifice that forms the soul for this body and is responsible for what I am today. I am eternally grateful to them for all that they have done for me.

Most of all, I thank lord almighty for the blessings showered upon me, which enabled me to complete this thesis work.

Saikumar B.C.
Berlin, August, 2009

Abstract

For India, as an agrarian economy, rural development *vis-a-vis* poverty alleviation has been considered a major challenge to the country. Microcredit through SHGs has emerged as a springboard to reach the rural poor in order to meet their financial demands. The peer group pressure is identified as a valuable collateral substitute and resulted in highest repayment. Presently, microcredit through Self-Help Groups (SHGs) in India is being practiced in different ways and is grouped and monitored under three models based on their linkage with the supporting institution – Model-I: Bank-promoted; Model-II: government agency; and Model-III: NGO-promoted. Since each of these models is operating under a different framework of rules and regulations, they also differ in their performance and observe wide variations in the percentage of their population coverage. Thus, the present study attempts to examine the factors influencing the performance and collective action of these three microcredit delivery models. The primary data was collected in three *taluks* of the Davanagere district in the state of Karnataka, India. In a multistage random sampling, three SHGs from each microcredit model were randomly selected from a total sample of nine SHGs. Ten members from each SHG, and thus a total of 90 members, were randomly interviewed. It is clear from the findings of factor analysis that there are several factors influencing the performance of SHGs. The results reveal that the direction and magnitude of variance of each variable in explaining the factor loadings of the components varies from one model to another. Loan repayment status and overall group functioning are used as dependent variables to measure the economic and social performance respectively using correlation, multinomial logistic (MNL) regression, and categorical regression analysis. The correlation analysis showed that several social and economic variables showed different patterns of relationships with loan repayment status and, in turn, in economic performance of SHGs in all three models. The MNL regression revealed that in Model-I, the amount of savings in the SHG per person, the loan amount taken per person, and satisfaction with the workings of the supporting institution are the important factors influencing the repayment status. In Model-II, with the exception of the age of the SHG and satisfaction with the workings of the supporting institution, all other predictors influence the economic performance. In Model-III, all the variables significantly influence the economic performance except for the age of the SHG. Furthermore, categorical regression analysis revealed that many factors influence the social performance of the SHGs at different levels under the three microcredit models. The findings of the curve-estimation technique for the selected structural variables, like homogeneity of the group, age of the SHGs, and freedom of participation with collective action, revealed that the level of the collective action is different across the three models and differs from the variation in the structural variables. From the overall study, it is observed that SHGs in Model-I perform better than SHGs of the other two models. Based on the results obtained, important variables are identified, consolidated, and mapped as social, economic, and institutional factors for a sustainable microcredit model. Hence, emphasis should be given for these variables for better performance of the SHGs, irrespective of the microcredit models.

Abbreviations

SHGs	Self-Help Groups
NGOs	Non-Governmental Organisations
WCDD	Women and Child Development Department
INR	Indian Rupees
SC/ST	Schedule Caste / Schedule Tribe
OBC	Other Backward Caste
MNL regression	Multinomial logistic regression
NABARD	National Bank for Agriculture and Rural Development
RBI	Reserve Bank of India
RRBs	Regional Rural Banks
MFI	Microfinance Institutions
IGA	Income-Generating Activities
CGAP	Consultative Group to Assist the Poorest
Tq	*Taluk*
ROSCAs	Rotating and Savings Credit Associations
CEEC	Central and Eastern European Countries
OLS	Ordinary Least Squares
LR	Likelihood Ratio
Conventions:	
Model-I	Bank-promoted SHGs
Model-II	Government agency (*Sthree Shakti*)
Model-III	NGO-promoted

Table of contents

List of Tables

List of figures

Chapter 1 Introduction

1.1. Overview of rural India

The prosperity of India lies in the prosperity of its villages. In spite of being an agrarian economy, India's rural sector reveals a despondent picture (BARDHAN and DABAS, 2007). Hence, in India – right from its independence, in fact even in the pre-independence era – rural development vis-a-vis poverty alleviation had been considered as a major challenge to the country (ATHENA, 2009). In fact, one in five of the world's people live in absolute poverty – two-third of them are women (STATE FOR INTERNATIONAL DEVELOPMENT REPORT, 2000). There are estimated to be about 1.2 billion people in the world who are blighted by poverty and are unable to meet their basic needs of food, clothing, shelter, and acquire minimum health care. Today, India retains the dubious distinction of having the largest number of poor people on the planet, where almost three out of four Indians and close to 80 per cent of the poor live in rural areas (HANSTAD *et al.*, 2002), in which 77 per cent (836 million) live on less than half a dollar a day (2009).[1] Though the Indian economy is witnessing GDP growth rates of 6.5 to 7.0 per cent, and despite the significant growth in agricultural production and employment over the past five decades, one out of every three persons in India is poor and two out of every three are undernourished or malnourished. If we include those who are deprived of safe drinking water, adequate clothing, or shelter, the number is considerably higher. Though the percentage of poverty has been reduced in India since 1947, the absolute numbers of poor who are still below the poverty line has doubled to about 300 millions. About 28.30 per cent of the population in rural areas and 25.70 per cent in urban areas live below the poverty line (PLANNING COMMISSION, 2007).

There are about 0.638 million villages in India and 75 per cent of the total population lives in rural areas, of which 68 per cent of the population depends on agriculture for their livelihood. The rural sector is typically characterised by subdivisions and fragmentation of landholding, which encourages underemployment, malnutrition, poverty, and results in lack of financial resources, leading to increased poverty. Thus, poverty in India is associated with an imbalance between the

1 http://www.expressindia.com/news/print.php?newsid=90717, accessed on 20 June 2009.

population and land resources. Landless and near-landless sections of the population live close to the margins of existence, experiencing seasonal unemployment and nutritional stress under severe poverty. Seeing the burden of poverty that falls heavily upon women, *Pandit Jawaharalal Nehru* (The first prime minister of India) envisioned that women can be the driving force to eradicate poverty. This sentiment is reflected very well in one of his statements, "When women move forward, the family moves, the village moves and the nation moves." Witnessing this, presently more than 90 per cent of SHGs are women groups showing tremendous progress in extending microcredit to the vulnerable (GOVERNMENT OF INDIA, 2007).

1.2. Emergence of microcredit in rural India

The need for rural credit in India had been recognised even before independence by the erstwhile British government as early as 1793, when it issued regulations for *taccavi* loans to farmers and subordinate tenants for various purposes (GOVERNMENT OF JHARKHAND, 2007). Measures were initiated to reduce indebtedness and regulate money-lending activities for agricultural purposes, but it failed to provide a long-term solution. The Co-operative Societies Act, which was passed in 1904 to provide necessary legislative support for financing agriculture and for regulating credit in the interest of cultivators, signalled the entry of credit for agriculture from the institutional sector. These cooperatives are formal organisations that were started long before the concept of SHGs in India, but were based on similar principles as neighbourhood groups or thrift-oriented, member-led, autonomous organisations, etc. Since then and till the late 1950s, cooperatives have been the major institutional source for all agricultural loans in rural areas. At that time, it focussed only on ensuring production credit loans for farmers through primary credit societies. But for non-farm credit needs, farmers paid very high interest rates to private moneylenders. As a result it became difficult for the poor to access funds for starting even small income-generation activities like tailoring, buying buffalo, goat- and sheep-rearing, and petty shop business for self-consumption needs, etc.

Later, for the first time, the Syndicate Bank, which started functioning in 1921, concentrated on raising micro-deposits as daily or weekly savings and providing micro-loans for its constituents. After the nationalisation of banks in 1969, the microfinance concept in the banking institutions was discussed once again. Despite having a broad network of bank branches in the rural parts of the country, a large number of the poor remained outside the fold of the formal banking system. On average, there is at least one retail credit for about every 5,000 people in the rural population – or for every 1,000 households – and the rural credit share from non-institutional sources (informal credit) is more than 36 per cent (GOVERNMENT OF JHARKHAND, 2007), indicating the role of moneylenders in the rural credit system and also highlighting that India is home to a growing and innovative sector for microcredit.

The structure of rural financial markets in India is dualistic, with formal, semi-formal, and informal intermediaries such as:

- **Formal Sector MFIs:** These include private and public institutions that are funded by government or foreign capital. The transactions involve some bureaucratic procedures with a bias for larger loans, for example, the commercial and cooperative banks, state-owned rural banks.
- **Semi-Formal MFIs:** These are not regulated by banks, but usually licensed and supervised by donor or government agencies that fund such institutions. These include some NGOs, credit unions.
- **Informal Sector MFIs:** These operate outside the structure of government regulation or supervision, including many Self-Help Groups and NGOs supporting micro enterprises.

The study by Adolph (2003) emphasised that the formal financial market failed in effectively serving the rural population in fulfilling their basic functions such as:

- Production credit to finance income-generating activities;
- Consumption credit to maintain and expand human productive capacity;
- Micro-saving schemes for increasing risk-bearing capacity of the rural households.

In fact, the cooperative credit was introduced in India as a defence mechanism against the exploitation of the rural poor. However, with the growth of cooperatives as formal organisations, they have ceased to be thrift-oriented, member-led, and autonomous organisations. Though conceptually the rich and the poor members can participate equally in the cooperative effort, the needs of the poor often get marginalised (PANDA and MISHRA, 1996). As a result, the performance of formal cooperative credit institutions – particularly with respect to rural India – has been unsatisfactory.

Later, the microcredit system gained momentum in the mid-1990s after the World Summit for Social Development,[2] held in Copenhagen in 1995. The summit – which emphasised the easy access to credit for small producers, landless farmers, and other low-income individuals, particularly women – urged governments of various nations to take appropriate actions in order to provide easy accessibility to credit by the poor. Subsequently, in 1997, the Microcredit Summit in Washington, DC, announced a global target of ensuring delivery of credit to 100 million of the world's poorest families, especially to the women of those families, by 2005. In the past, despite the vast institutional credit network, the attempt to serve the weaker section of society, particularly women and the deprived, had yielded only limited success (GABA and ABHA, 2003; JUSTUS and MOHIBA, 2000). Microcredit Summit 2006 set goals to be reached by 2015 that were aimed at: 1) reaching 175 million of the poorest families with microcredit; 2) ensuring that 100 million families rise above the US$1-a-day threshold, which would lift 500 million people out of extreme poverty (UNFPA, 2006). To reach the summit goal of 100 million families, each country must reach 50 per cent of the poor families in their country. As a solution to overcoming the previous limitations and to achieve the target, SHGs are used as a springboard to reach the rural poor to help them meet their financial demands in the present world (ROY, 1994; OJHA, 2001).

1.3. Origin of Self-Help Groups

SHGs in their basic form existed in rural society long prior to the period when rural planners formulated this concept. The groups have also been termed "affinity groups" due to the existing natural bonds of neighbourhood, blood, caste, community, or activity, as well as being termed "solidarity groups", as they provide monetary and moral support to each other in difficult times. SHG is not a new concept in Indian society. Traditional Indian society functioned mainly on the basis of self-help and mutual aid. However, in recent years, SHGs have been emerging as a major strategy for the promotion of informal credit to the poor. The concept of SHG in India can be traced back to the Gandhian Grama Swaraj movement. It is mainly concerned with

2 http://www.un.org/documents/ga/conf166/aconf166-9.htm.

the poor and helping each other through the motto, "Of the people and for the people". Unlike many other countries that implemented SHGs after the mid-1970s as a part of the formal credit delivery system, India has been experimenting with the concept for decades (KARMAKAR, 1998).

However, the origins of SHGs in their present form can be traced back as the brain child of Grameen Bank of Bangladesh, founded by Prof Mohammed Yunus of Chittagong University, Bangladesh, in the year 1975 (JAYARAMAN, 2001). This innovation has proved that credit is not only for the privilege of a few fortunate people, but that the poor and vulnerable can also afford it to assist in their development. This argument of Prof Mohammed Yunus, which acknowledges people's human rights and offers a unique vision, merited him a Nobel Prize. In fact, the dependence of the rural poor on non-institutional sources of credit like moneylenders is one of the major causes perpetuating poverty. SHGs are identified as substitutes and an antidote for that poverty. In Bangladesh, it has developed into a national programme and has shown remarkable results regarding poverty mitigation. These SHGs have emerged as alternative credit sources for the poor with the recovery performance of 99 per cent, with mutual trust, solidarity, group accountability, and collective action as inherent operational mechanisms (RAJAGOPALAN, 1998). Indeed, the impetus of the present-day SHG movement can be attributed to the success of the Grameen Bank. Presently, it functions in over 52 countries and has been operational for a long time in Bangladesh, Malaysia, Korea, Philippines, and Indonesia.

In Indian rural villages, neighbourhood groups are informally named with different local names but widely known as Self-Help Groups. These are informal groups of 10 to 20 members who have a common vision of the need and importance of collective action (KHUN, 1985). These groups promote savings among members and use the pooled resources to meet the emergency needs of their members, including consumption needs. It is obvious that collective work, leadership with fixed tenure, mutual trust, and cooperative philosophy would be the underlying driving forces for these SHGs. The basic tenet of SHGs is to develop savings capabilities among the poorest sections of the society, which in turn reduces dependence on financial institutions and thereby develops self-reliance. However, unlike savings activities found in SHGs of several other countries, these SHG's in India also obtain loans from microfinance banking institutions and then re-lend them to the members of the group. Thus microcredit through SHGs has become a fulcrum for developmental initiatives for the poor, particularly in India and in developing countries. It has been practiced in varying forms in different countries and it has been regarded as an important tool for poverty alleviation.

1.4. Progress of SHGs microfinance models in India

Self-Help Groups are voluntary groups that come together to obtain loans from financial institutions in order to meet their financial needs to improve standards of living. It is seen as a good means both from the perspective of group members, who do not have direct access to bank loans, and also from the viewpoint of financial institutions regarding recovery success, since members with loans will experience neighbourhood (group) pressure to repay loans. In many of the cases, microcredit has helped Self-Help Groups to start self-employment projects in groups as well. Thus since last decade, SHG banking is the primary mode of microfinance in India. Today, financing through SHGs is becoming the best medium to include the rural poor in the formal financial sector. Reaching over six million families presently in India, the following three models have primarily evolved for the purpose of linking SHGs with banks (ADOLPH, 2003; ROBERT, 2005).

Model-I – SHGs formed and financed directly by banks **(Bank-promoted)**:

In this model, the SHGs are organised and promoted directly by banks. Banks provide credit in bulk directly to the SHG, which might be an informal or registered body. Then, SHGs would lend to its members with terms and conditions. NABARD[3] provided refinance assistance to the lending banks. In this model there was no involvement of NGOs.

Model-II – SHGs formed by other agencies but directly financed by banks **(government department)**:

In this model, government agencies organise and promote the SHGs and then refer those SHGs to the bank for lending either to the SHGs or directly to individual members of the SHGs. The government agency stands only as a support to both the

3 The National Bank for Agricultural and Rural Development (NABARD) is an apex bank for rural development in India. It is accredited with all matters concerning policy, planning, and operations related to credit for agriculture and economic activities in rural areas.

bank and the SHGs for monitoring and evaluating the projects, the proper functioning of the SHGs, the repayment of the loans, the training of members of SHGs, etc.

Model-III – SHGs, financed by banks but NGOs, act as financial intermediaries **(NGO-promoted)**:

Here, the SHGs are organised and promoted by NGOs and referred to the bank for linkage and the bank provides finance directly to the NGO for lending to the SHGs or to individual members of the SHGs. NGO will be fully responsible for making repayment to the bank and it also performs the functions that are in Model-II.

In India the first effort was taken up by the National Bank for Agriculture and Rural Development (NABARD) in 1986/87 on a pilot basis, and then the concept of SHGs for banking, finance, and development was prepared by the Reserve Bank of India (RBI) from 1991 onwards. Later NABARD launched a project to provide microcredit by linking SHGs with the bank after 1991/92 (NABARD, 1995). In a research study (NABARD, 2007) it is stated that from a modest beginning in 1992/93 with 255 SHGs in 10 states, the number of SHGs increased substantially by a hundredfold, to 0.717 million in 2002/03, covering all states and union territories. Cumulatively, 0.717 million SHGs were provided microfinance loan aggregating Indian Rupees (INR)[4] 20,487.00 million, benefiting 7.8 million poor households in India. Total microfinance loans disbursed to SHGs during 2003 are aggregated to INR 10,223.00 million involving a refinance of INR 6,223.00 million by the national banks. Recent statistics based on a Government of India report on SHGs and microfinance in 2007 is presented in Table 1. In the table we can see that more than 90 per cent of the financed groups are women-run SHGs, which amount to about 2.92 million. This covers about 40.95 million poor household families, i.e., an 18 per cent growth in outreach to rural areas (SRINIVASAN, 2008).

In spite of its considerable outreach, successful savings mobilisation, and high repayment rates, as with most other microfinance models the financial viability of SHG banking has not been clear due to dualistic participation of both formal and informal institutions. The graph below indicates the share of three models in microfinance delivery that are in wide practice in India.

4 The currency exchange rate of euro to INR is 1 euro = 65 Indian rupees.

Table 1. SHGs' progress highlights in India

Sl. No.	Particulars	Data
1	No. of SHGs microfinanced (million)	2.924
2	% of women groups	90%
3	No. of participating banks	498
	1.Commercial banks	50
	2. RRBs	96
	3. Cooperative banks	352
4	No. of states/UTs	31
5	No. of districts covered	587
6	Bank loan INR in billion	180.41
7	Refinance INR in billion	54.59
8	No. of poor households assisted (in millions)	40.95
9	Average loan (INR)/SHG	
	New SHGs	44,342
	Repeat	78,693
10	Average Loan(INR)/Family	
	New	3,167
	Repeat	5,621

Source: Government of India, 2007.

Fig 1. Model-wise share in delivery of microfinance (%) in India

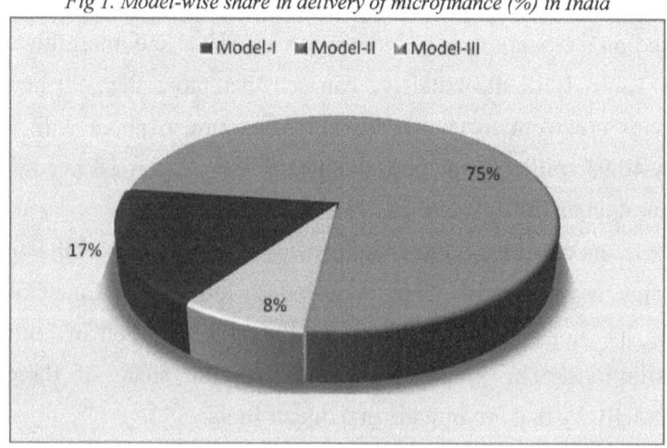

Source: NABARD Report, 2007.

Figure 1 indicates that there is wide variation in the shares of the implemented models in India, where Model-II covers about 75 per cent of SHGs, Model-I about 17 per cent, and the remaining 8 per cent of SHG micro financing is done through Model-III (GOVERNMENT OF KERALA, 2004). The above models operate under different frameworks of rules and regulations; they also differ in the amount of government support, purpose of loan, amount of loan disbursement, interest rate, mode of repayment, etc. Numerous studies have been conducted on the impact of microfinance and SHGs and the performance of each individual model, and each of these models has been found to have varying positive impacts from an objective point of view in an Indian context. But there has been no attempt to compare the performances between these three models.

1.5. Problem statement

The turn of the century was marked by significant and promising events intended to tackle challenges for world development. About 189 countries in the year 2000 signed on to the Millennium Development Goals, with poverty eradication being one of the main targets (GLOBAL MONITORING REPORT, 2004). One in two children born in the world lives in poverty. Of the world's 6 billion people, 2.8 billion live on less than $2 a day and 1.2 billion live on less than $1 a day. Of these 1.2 billion, 500 million live in south Asia. The World Bank (WORLD BANK DEVELOPMENT REPORT, 2008) reported a decline in the rural poverty rate in developing countries, from 28 per cent in 1993 to 22 per cent in 2002, whereas the urban poverty rate has remained nearly constant at about 13 per cent, indicating that urban migration is not the solution for poverty eradication. However, poverty still persists strongly in rural areas of developing countries, posing us a challenge to tackle poverty in rural areas and to make poverty history, at least in the future.

Being a largely populated country, India is one of the developing countries facing the serious challenge of poverty. Since independence though, the government has initiated, sustained, and implemented various poverty-eradication programmes, as per the study by the National Commission for Enterprises in the Unorganised Sector (NCEUS, 2007), and though it is one of the world's hottest economies, about 77 per cent of the population (836 million) lives on less than half a dollar a day. Martin J. Cetro, founder and analysts of Forecast International (MARTIN, 2004), estimates that

300 million Indians now belong to the middle class, of which one-third of them have emerged from poverty in the last 10 years. Currently 40 million people are added to the middle class every year. At the current rate of growth, a majority of Indians will be middle class by 2025. The proportion of India's population that lies below the poverty line has fluctuated widely in the past, but the overall trend is downward. According to Planning Commission and NSSO Data (NSSO, 2006), the poverty ratio over the period has shown a significant downward trend in India: from 56.40 per cent in 1973/74 to the present level of 27.50 per cent. But in absolute terms, 193 million rural people are in perpetual bondage to poverty (BARDHAN and DABAS, 2007), making the issue of poverty a momentous challenge for development, both in the near future and in the long run (NCEUS, 2007).

One of the major causes of poverty in rural India is the lack of access to productive assets and financial resources for both individuals and communities (NAILA, 2005). Most of the rural poor are small and marginal or landless farmers who do not have access to a banking system or any formal financial support system and mainly dependent on agriculture for their livelihoods. A study (WORLD BANK, 1995) revealed that 67 per cent of the credit needed by the poor in India was for consumption needs; of the consumption credit required, 75 per cent was for short periods for emergent needs such as illness and household expenses during the lean monsoon seasons. It was also estimated that 75 per cent of production credit (only 33% of total credit) was met by banks while 100 per cent of the consumption-credit requirement was met by informal resources at very high interest rates ranging from 30 to 90 per cent per annum. Unfortunately, a majority of the farmers who are cash-starved, due to lack of credit, are unable to adopt most of the new technologies that can give them more income. The International Fund for Agricultural Development noted that over a billion poor people lack access to basic financial services, which are essential for them to manage their lives (IFAD, 2007). The main factors acting as barriers to credit access from the borrower's side are: deficient or inappropriate collateral credit-rationing; high transaction cost; lender preferences for high-income customers borrowing large amounts; and long bureaucratic procedures in the formal financial sector. All these together are identified as key factors contributing to low access to formal credit among the rural dwellers. Thus, lack of money, low return, diversified and subsistence-oriented production practices, and indebtedness to private moneylenders due to their high interest rates creates the vicious cycle of poverty. In the study conducted by the Gupta committee in the year 1996, barriers from the bank's side in reaching out to the poorer sections of society are: the transaction costs inherent in servicing small loans to a large number of borrowers; and the perceived risk cost in the absence of appropriate risk-management system.

While dealing with such broad, challenging scenario relating to indebtedness of small, marginal farmers and the poorest of the poor in the developing countries of the world in the mid-1980s, new innovations for accessing credit was found – it was called "microcredit". Microcredit primarily meets the strong demand for small-scale commercial financial services, such as credit and savings. Thus, in the development of a new paradigm, microfinance is recognised as a promising and effective tool in fighting poverty and seen as a needs-based policy programme to cater to the thus far neglected target groups (like the poorest of the poor, women, landless labourers, the deprived, etc.) by providing financial services to those who do not have access to commercial banks and financial institutions. The basic idea behind it is simple: If poor people are provided access to financial services, including credit (UNFPA, 2006), they may very well be able to start or expand a micro-enterprise that will allow them to escape the vicious poverty cycle.

According to UNESCO in the year 2004, about 67.6 million people around the world are estimated to have access to microfinance, and the number is estimated to cross 100 million by 2010 (UNESCO, 2004). Thus, microfinance has generated greater interest, enthusiasm, and worldwide attention among the international institutions, organisations, and development agencies at the world level against the successful background of the Bangladeshi Grameen Bank in offering microcredit to the rural poor. Meanwhile, the UN Year of Microcredit in 2005 signalled a turning point for microfinance as the private sector began to take a more serious interest in what had been considered the domain of NGOs. However, with all the excitement about the prospects of this field being able to contribute to poverty alleviation and the integration of the world's poor into the rapidly evolving global market system, the Consultative Group to Assist the Poorest (CGAP) estimated that microcredit probably reaches fewer than 5 per cent of its potential clients (CGAP, 2005), indicating enormous scope for the expansion of microcredit programmes to remote rural areas in the future.

In the beginning in India, this approach was extensively used by voluntary agencies (NGOs) for a long time, and then incorporated into the conventional development programmes only at the beginning of present decade (QAZI, 1999). In India, SHGs are grouped into three models[5] (Model-I: bank-promoted, Model-II: government agency, and Model-III: NGO-promoted) as described earlier, and they operate under different frameworks of rules and regulations, even starting from group formation. They also differ with regard to government support, purpose of loan, amount of loan disbursement, interest rate, mode of repayment, purpose, functioning, etc., (UNESCO, 2004) and hence also differ in their performance and impact on its members. Among these three models, Model-II has a much wider implementation compared to the other two models, which might be due to the large size of the programme implemented by the government. It indeed put forth an open question as which model performs better and it was decided to take up further research. There are numerous research studies that have been conducted and reflect positively on SHGs and their impact on socio-economic conditions of its members, basically the rural poor. There are also studies on the impact of microfinance and SHGs, and each one of these found that SHGs have varying positive impacts, regarding both their objective and institutional viability. Based on the rapid success made over the years, the programme was extended across the entire country under three delivery models to reach the rural poor at their doorstep. In terms of its outreach, it is now the largest microfinance programme in the world. Thus it was found that microfinance through Self-Help Groups is becoming one of the important means for eradicating poverty in the present context. But still there exists a high percentage of poverty in rural India. So, the next question will be to assess the comparative performance and collective action of these different models for their group capability, concert, and sustainability to tackle poverty in long run by further penetrating into the rural areas on a large scale and to attain comprehensive self-stability and sustainability by the rural poor through SHGs to make poverty history.

Moreover, among the three models, though, there are wide differences in the percentage of SHGs covered under microcredit, but no attempts were made to create comparative studies of these three microcredit delivery models at the SHG level with respect to the factors that influence the performance of SHGs and also collective

5 http://www.nabard.org/roles/mcid/shgbanklink.htm.

action, which is a key principle behind these SHGs. Thus, with this background, the present topic focuses on having an in-depth study on the performance of Self-Help Group microcredit delivery models and collective action – which are a must for the sustainable existence of rural development in the future – by offering the following key questions to the researchers.

Research questions:

- Which are the factors influencing the performance of microcredit delivery models of Self-Help Groups?
- How does performance vary with variation in different factors involved in the three SHG microcredit delivery models?
- How does the collective action differ among microcredit models at the Self-Help Group level?

1.6. Study goals

Based on present needs, this is the right time to have a study on the comparative performance of Self-Help Groups under these three models in order to determine the best one for helping with the further expansion of the programme. The implications drawn from the study will certainly help the policymakers while designing the developmental plans for rural areas in the future. With this background, the following objectives were fixed tentatively under the research study entitled "The Performance of Microcredit Organisations – A Comparative Perspective."

1.6.1. Research objectives

1. To study and compare the factors influencing the performance of different microcredit delivery models of SHGs by using multivariate techniques.
2. To study the collective action and structural variables[6] in different microcredit delivery models at the SHG level.

6 Structural variables include age of the group, homogeneity of the group, freedom of participation etc. (LICHBACH, 1996; OSTROM, 2001).

1.6.2. Hypotheses

1. The factors influencing the performance of SHGs differ from one model to another.
2. The performance of SHGs from Model-I is better than the performance of SHGs of the other two microcredit delivery models.
3. As structural variables change, collective action differs in the microcredit delivery models and drives the difference in their performance at the SHG level.

1.7. Structure of the thesis

The thesis is outlined in five main chapters. The first chapter starts with a brief introduction of India in general and the evolution of rural financial institutions in particular. Also, this includes the origin of SHGs and progress of SHG models in India, problem statement, study goals, research questions, objectives, and hypotheses. In the second chapter, review of literature is narrowed in general to the concept of SHG and further specified to its objectives. The third chapter mainly focuses on methodology, including salient features of the study area, sampling framework, analytical tools, and techniques. Based on knowledge gained from the review of literature and primary data, empirical results and discussions are presented in the fourth chapter. The fifth chapter summarises the whole research work carried out in order to derive conclusions from the research findings. This is followed by implications of the study, further research scope, and ends with limitations of the present study.

Chapter 2 Definitions, Concepts and Review of Literature

"Money, says the proverb, makes money. When you have got a little, it is often easy to get more. The great difficulty is to get that little."

-*ADAM SMITH*

In this chapter, an attempt has been made to explain certain concepts used in this study. In addition, this part is intended to critically review the literature of the past research work relevant to the present study objective, so that theoretical views and empirical evidence of the reviews can provide a better understanding of the subject.

2.1. Concepts and theoretical explanations

2.1.1. Poverty

Though "globalisation" and "global village" are discussed at the world level, poverty is still a major curse faced by many countries. The word "poverty" has a number of definitions – it is not easy to give an absolute definition and has relative definitions that depend on the situation. If we see some of the important definitions used globally, poverty, according to the CGAP report (CGAP, 2005), can be defined as "The proportion of population living below $1 a day (PPP)[7] or is the percentage of the population living on less than $1.08 a day at 1993 international prices." Whereas poverty is defined by the World Bank (WORLD BANK, 2000) as the condition of poor households or persons – interpreted conventionally as those lacking access to the assets necessary for a higher standard of income or welfare – assets are thought of as human (access to education), natural (access to land), physical (access to infrastructure), social (access to networks of obligations), or financial (access to credit). Thus, poverty has a relative definition confined to the particular environment and situation. In order to eradicate poverty, a number of programmes for free education, free health, and food-for-work programmes, etc., have been implemented

7 Purchasing Power Parities (PPPs) are currency conversion rates that both convert to a common currency and equalise the purchasing power of different currencies. In other words, they eliminate the differences in price levels between countries in the process of conversion. (Source: http://www.oecd.org/department/0,3355,en_2649_34357_1_1_1_1_1,00.html.)

globally. Lessons from these experiences is that these programmes did not fix the predicament, and when the quandary was analysed by experts, it led to the evolution of microcredit as an alternative means for poverty eradication. Later in the beginning of this decade, microcredit revolution has made to achieve progress in this facet. The next question is how microcredit has helped poverty alleviation. A study by ELLERMAN (2008) answers the question, wherein microcredit is described as being mainly sustaining those at the brink of survival who have low savings and no investments. Hence, the credit rarely re-enters the production capital, which can contribute meaningfully to farm growth. He further argues that targeting vulnerable, asset-less, non-entrepreneurial farmers who lack clear business ideas may help them to escape the vicious cycle of poverty. Thus, from the last decade onward, it is being realised that instead of targeting individuals, it is more advantageous from many perspectives to target the group. Currently, "microcredit" is recognised as an effective tool to fight poverty from the bottom-up approach in society (NEILS and ROBERT , 2007). Hence in recent years, SHGs have become the significant means of reaching the microcredit target group at the world level.

2.1.2. Definition and concept of Self-Help Groups

Basically, Self Help Groups, in essence are a form of cooperation with a definite ambience of dynamism and cohesion, collective action surfaced in the group members by their association within and outside the groups which are formed in their neighbourhood. There are different definitions given by different experts for the SHG concept and a few are presented below.

SHG is not a new concept in development. SHGs are the grassroots-level organisations that are based on the principles of need and collective action. While explaining about SHGs and its members, Harper said that an SHG is not a static institution (HARPER, 1996). It grows on resources and management skills of its members and their increasing confidence to get involved in issues and programmes that require their involvement in the public and private sectors. Through an SHG, the members are automatically empowered economically, politically, and socially in a holistic way for developing their own institution for common benefit. Many studies have shown that creating savings through thrift and credit has been one of the important activities of SHGs, and it became very popular among the poor, particularly among women in the rural areas (KUMARAN, 1997). However, SHGs cannot be considered as credit or savings groups alone; they also conduct the mobilisation and organisation of women into groups, because these groups form the basis for solidarity, strength, and collective action (KHUN, 1985). Organising such groups has a way to go yet in addressing not only economic problems but also social and political issues.

Author	Definition
HAGENBUCH (1958)	SHGs are mutual help organisations formed by a group of people to help each other and are essentially democratic in nature.
CHAWLA and PATEL (1987)	Self-Help organisations are entities that are set up and run by local people who are also the beneficiaries of the programme; it has a loose organisational structure but strong commitment and sense of purpose.
ROYAL TROPICAL INSTITUTE (1987)	SHG is a membership organisation or group wherein risks, costs, and benefits are shared among its members on an equitable basis; its leadership and managers are liable to be called to account by the membership for their needs.
SINGH (1995)	SHG is an informal association of individuals who come together voluntarily for promotion of economic and social objectives.
ROUL (1996a)	SHG is an institutional framework for individuals or households who have agreed to cooperate on a continuing basis to pursue one or more objectives.
INDIAN BANK (1996)	SHG is a homogenous group of not more than 25 individuals who have come together to undertake thrift and credit for economic and social strength on the basis of equality, nurturing trust, and mutual help.

These groups were first organised as savings groups for women to overcome the lack of credit access for their needs. Once the group is able to accumulate the sufficient amount of money, it will be encouraged to take up various income-generating activities, either as a form of group initiative or as an activity of the individual member. The money saved by women is used not only for meeting their emergent consumption needs but also for income-generating activities (RAO, 1994).

2.1.3. Microcredit

The microcredit concept was first introduced in Bangladesh for experiment in the 1950s and 60s; since then, all government efforts to empower peasants' households failed in the late 1970s and 80s. It led to the emergence of a new microcredit lending programme by the Bangladesh Grameen Bank and Bangladesh Rural Advancement Committee[8] in the 1980s to reach poor landless households. Beneficiaries of the microcredit loans were poor women who did not have assets to present as collateral in banks and hence never had access to formal banking institutions before (JAYARAMAN, 2001). One important feature of microcredit is that it gives credit "based on trust" without any collateral security. Even then it has achieved on average more than 90 per cent credit recovery. Literature confirms that this success is mainly because of group-lending, where each group member experiences pressure from the neighbourhood regarding loan repayment (SA-DHAN, 2008). In Bangladesh most of the microcredit funds were put towards paddy husking, livestock rearing, aquaculture, vegetable production, poultry farming, and petty business. In another study, the researcher LEDGERWOOD (1999) enunciated that microcredit is not just a credit, but it is also a development tool that involves activities such as small loans (microcredit) for working capital, informal assessment of borrowers and investments, collateral substitutes (group guarantees or compulsory savings), and access to subsequent loans based on repayment performance. In fact, microcredit groups are used for a range of activities at the world level. In India Self-Employed Women's Association – which has given microcredit for strong social components like labour advocacy, health care, and education – proves that microcredit groups can be expanded to any extent based on successful participation of rural households.

The concept of microcredit has emerged and expanded, going beyond Asia, America, and Africa and even reaching Eastern Europe in the name of microfinance

8 Bangladesh Rural Advancement Committee (BRAC) was established in the year 1970 on pilot basis and became an NGO and was implemented in many developing countries.

at Mercy Corps[9] at the world level. Professor Muhammad Yunus launched a €150 million global microfinance outfit styled by Grameen-Credit Agricole Foundation in Paris on 18 February 2008. Credit Agricole SA and Grameen Trust have teamed up to create a dedicated foundation (STAR, 2008). It is intended to provide microfinance institutions with a complete range of financing facilities in the form of credits, guarantees, and equity capital along with advisory services. Grameen Trust is a sister organisation of Grameen Bank, which stepped in to support microfinance initiatives in 38 countries. In China, the Chinese Foundation for Poverty Alleviation[10] in Beijing – a government NGO under the State Poverty Alleviation Office – developed successfully its own microcredit model based on the Grameen Bank model. Mercy Corps is another important organisation supporting microcredit in dozens of countries ravaged by wars, conflict, and civil unrest. By and large the microcredit experiment has been tried all over the world due to the problem of rising poverty. The Association of Social Advancement is an international NGO providing assistance to 30 organisations in 17 countries. One assisted organisation was also an NGO from India called Bandhan located in West Bengal, which had women as the primary borrowers. At the global level, the study conducted on the microcredit summit campaign reported that 1.6 million were served microcredit in the year 1997, but presently there are about 3,100 microfinance institutions providing microcredit to the 92.9 million poor people at the world level, indicating microcredit is no longer micro in its global approach (KABIR, 2002). Out of the 92.9 million people in the world, Asia's share is 59.6 million.

According to a study by Sa-Dhan (2007), India is performing well regarding microcredit, with a Compound Annual Growth Rate of 76 per cent. NABARD conducted research on the impact assessment of microcredit in 2005. It inferred that microfinance clients have diversified their risks and thus reduced the vulnerability to external factors and that they also were able to provide regular and more years of schooling to their children. Women were empowered in decision-making.

Following successes with microcredit, microcredit operations in India became the centre of discussion globally in 2002. Consequently, SHGs and microcredit are considered very essential for the complete eradication of poverty. On the other hand,

---

9 Mercy Corps is an international humanitarian aid and development charitable organisation that focuses on emergency relief services, economic development, and civil society.

10 http://www.cfpa.com.

researchers emphasise that, in context of the magnitude of poverty and flow of funds for poverty alleviation through microcredit, there has been very little intervention in India (THANKHA, 2002). Figure 2 explains the present outreach and scope for microcredit expansion in context of the depth and intensity of outreach in India.

Fig 2. Microfinance coverage in India

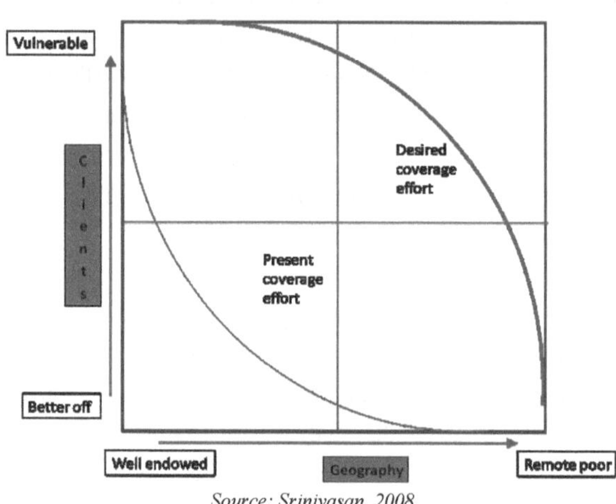

Source: Srinivasan, 2008

The above figure explains the distribution of the microfinance services across the country and also the coverage of the most vulnerable sections of population through SHGs. In terms of its coverage of the poor clients, the four southern states in India, namely Tamil Nadu, Karnataka, Andhra Pradesh, and Kerala, which have made outstanding progress in SHG credit linkage, have reached both targeted groups: the upper strata of poor and the ultra poor. In the other six major north Indian states, there are very few clients, constituting less than 1 per cent of the total clients. In terms of geographical coverage, well-endowed and high-growth areas have been prioritised. The expansion within such areas has also not been consciously targeted towards the poor. The most vulnerable are not clients of choice for most organisations engaged in SHG promotion or microfinance institution lending (MFI) in such areas. In poorly endowed, backward, and remote areas, even the better-off among the poor do not get covered, as these areas are not yet on the microfinance map. The critically poor remain excluded, indicating that a vast sample of the population is still waiting to harness micro financing benefits through SHGs to escape poverty.

Many research studies have proved that microcredit through SHGs seems impressive and found it to be one of the potential weapons for eradicating poverty in India. This necessitates in expounding on the institutional structure of the three microcredit delivery models of SHGs in reaching the poor in India – explained in figures 4, 5, and 6 (RAKESH MALHOTRA, 2005).

Fig 3. Model-I showing bank-promoted SHGs working structure

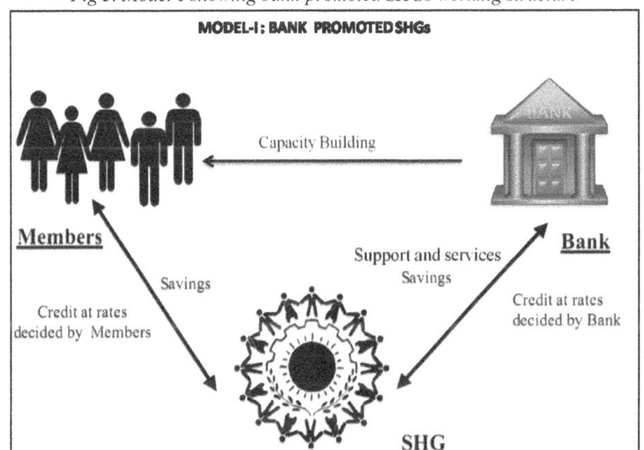

Bank-promoted (Model-I) SHGs are one of the three microcredit delivery models of SHGs operating explicitly in India. In this model, banks play a key role in all SHG activities. This model has succeeded in meeting the main objectives of microcredit and SHG programmes, both from an institutional perspective and from the member's side. The Consultative Group to Assist the Poor (CGAP) in its study (CGAP, 2007) recognises that the model has met the target of reaching the poor, and it might be due to directed lending and priority-sector quotas imposed on public sector commercial banks. Indian commercial banks, most of which are government-owned, began lending to SHGs because of government-imposed, priority-sector lending quotas (RBI, 2007). The fact is that lending via microfinance accounted for less than 1 per cent of the priority-sector lending done by banks and less than 0.40 per cent of total credit of commercial banks as of 31 March 2007, leaving a lot of scope for further expansion of the programme.

Fig 4. Model-II showing government agency-promoted SHGs working structure

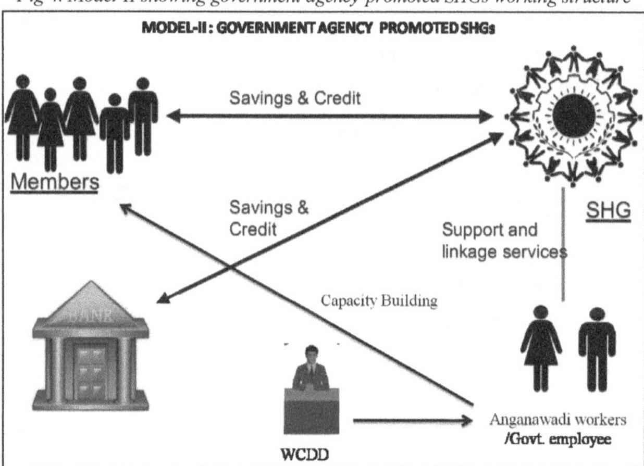

The second model of microcredit delivery by SHGs is through a government agency. It forms the group and facilitates linkages to the bank, training, capacity-building, and regular monitoring. The Government of India had come up with the *Sthree Shakti* (government agency)[11] scheme in 2000/01. It mainly supported the SHG movement in rural areas to empower women to fight against poverty and to assist rural women in understand their rights as well as gaining economic independence, freedom of participation, and access to credit. At the village level, school teachers (*Anganwadi* workers) are the grassroots workers from the government side; they work with SHGs with an objective to make members self-reliant and to achieve financial stability through neighbourhood Self-Help Groups.

11 http://wcd.nic.in/ and http://www.kar.nic.in/dwcd/.

Fig 5. Model-III showing NGO-promoted SHGs working structure

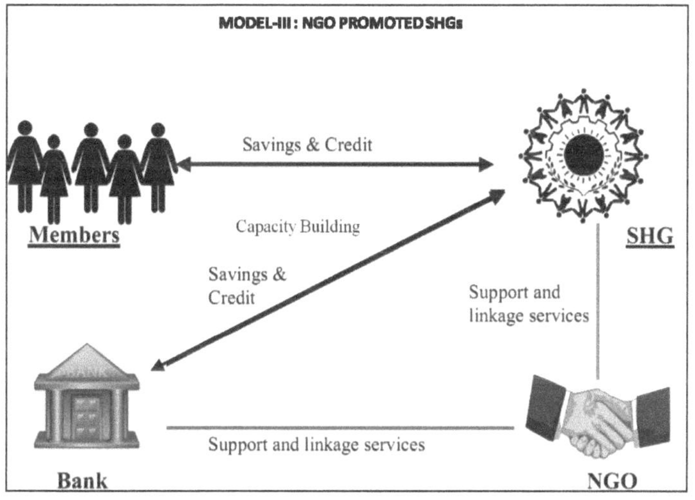

The third model includes microcredit delivery for the SHGs, which are formed by NGOs and linked to banks. In fact, the concept of NGOs (voluntary organisations) was already there in India from the early 19th century, when the country was still under the clutches of the British (SMITH and FREEDMAN, 1972). In the beginning, microcredit started only under the flagship Grameen Bank in Bangladesh; later NGOs emerged to fill the void left by the failure of banks to serve the poor effectively and have become the true pioneers at the world level (BRIGHT, 2006). As time advanced microcredit began being championed and monitored by thousands of NGOs around the globe, often combining small business training, consulting, and marketing support and then adopting different national governments as part of a development programme at the international level (SNOW and BUSS, 2001). In the same way in India, NGOs are playing a crucial role by providing their own ways for SHGs formation, bank linkage, support, and services through active and meaningful participation and thereby making an impact on rural members that is different from the other two models. Supporting this statement is the example of the Dhan Foundation working in India, which, along with giving credit to the poor, also provides training on income-generating activities like tailoring, hand looming, food processing, etc., so that the SHG members can develop their own livelihood strategy (SA-DHAN, 2007).

Fig 6. Commonality in inflow and outflow of SHGs

In all the three models, commonality in inflow and outflow of SHGs are …

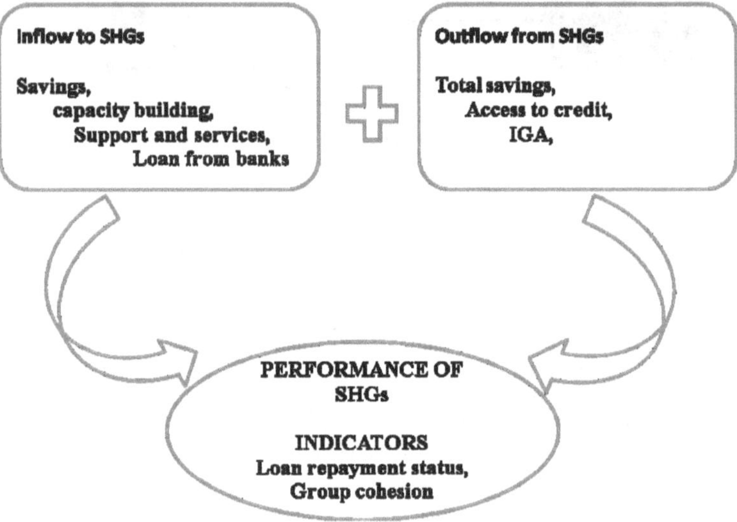

The Indian microcredit sector is known for its diversity of microcredit delivery models of SHGs. In India, SHGs of all three microcredit delivery models are working simultaneously with the same objectives and target group. But they diverge in their framework, approach, and execution and as well in performance (REDDY, 2007). In the above flowchart, we can see that all three models have few important common features in their functioning such as savings, capacity-building, support, and services, loan from bank linkages on inflow side to SHGs and on the outflow side they have total savings of the members and access to credit by the group, purpose of credit like income-generating activities (IGA) or other purposes. In all the models we can distinguish their performance from SHGs and its member's side in repayment status and group cohesion as economic and social performance indicators respectively. Further, using these indicators the three models can be compared to analyse and to find the better one, so that the results can assist for further improvement of the programme in vital direction. This encourages the emerging research in this direction to achieve success in explaining SHGs' microcredit for rural development.

2.2. Empirical studies on performance of SHG

There are quite a lot of studies that have been done on microcredit, SHGs, and poverty alleviation, as it has become the spring board for rural development. However, because of its deep penetration in terms of its outreach in the rural poor and importance gained at international and national levels, it has several horizons to do research from different perspectives. A few of the studies related to the study objectives are presented here.

2.2.1. Performance of Self-Help Groups

Self-Help Groups are organisations whose members have united on the basis of a common interest to improve their economic and social conditions in order to better attain their long-term aims (VERHAGEN, 1987). With this universal vision of SHGs in mind, many research studies have been done at the national and international levels focussing on microcredit through SHGs from various directions. In most of the developing countries, the provisions of small-size loans and other financial services to low-income households through SHGs is often seen as the key innovation of the last 25 years in terms of reaching out to the poor and vulnerable. Extensive experiences have been observed in Asia and Latin America, and to a lesser extent in China (HEATHER and WEISS, 2006). Researchers have attempted to assess the different approaches (models) of microfinance delivery using a threefold distinction – like the credit union approach, the NGO approach, and the banking approach – to generalise recent Asian and Latin American experiences. They have discussed the role of microfinance in poverty reduction in a theoretical framework that considers the current state of microfinance in China. The study suggests that the banking approach model is the best way in terms of outreach to the target groups in China.

An empirical analysis has been made on Rotating and Savings Credit Associations (ROSCAs)[12] in Senegal. The study mainly focussed on the cooperation, performance, and sustainability of ROSCAs with a set of variables that reflects group size, group heterogeneity, norms, and other various institutional designs (FADIGA and FADIGA STEWART, 2004). The performance of ROSCA is studied using log-linear regression with default rate as indicator of performance: The higher the default rate, the less effective the association. There are several variables considered in the analysis, like age dispersion of participants, gender composition, loan amount, age of ROSCA, size of the association, amount of savings per month by individual members, frequency of contribution, default history of members, ratio of number of defaults to size of association, reasons for default, measures to cover default. The results revealed that availability of default coverage and size of ROSCA contributes to increases in the default rate. The default rate is lower for same-gender composition association, associations with higher contribution levels, and those members who are offered help. Further, default rate increases by 0.41 per cent for each additional member in the group when all other variables were held constant. This study by researchers finally infers that the length of existence of an association, the coverage available to cover a default, and the association size all work to lower institutional performance, whereas the member homogeneity, individual contribution levels, and offers to help allowed for enhanced performance of the association.

In another analogous study on performance in the agriculture sector, LOUIS *et al.* (2002) did an investigation in Central and Eastern European Countries (CEEC) about government performance, institutional environment, government structures, and social capital, because they emphasise that there is a strong relationship between the determinants of good government performance and those for good government in realising sustainable agriculture. The study explained how common values and norms serve as a coordination principle for groups and it also explained how non-contractual elements like trust, social beliefs, and group cohesion – altogether called social capital – will influence the performance and sustainability of the government. In the study ordinary least squares (OLS) regression model and logistic regression were used to analyse the role of institutional, economical, and social capital factors in

12 The rotating savings and credit association (ROSCA) is an association in Africa formed upon a core of participants who all agree to make regular contributions to a fund that is given in whole or in part to each contributor in rotation in the group (ARDENER 1964, p. 201).

explaining why the agricultural sector in some countries has performed better than that in other CEECs. Results of the study showed that institutional elements and social capital are important variables that differ in different countries, thereby influencing their performance.

Presently, in a large country like India, several of the national rural development programmes implemented that are based on the SHG strategy necessitate an immediate addressing of questions related to the performance of different microcredit models of SHGs in order to know the viability of the model. A study (RENUKARYA, 2004) assessed the performance of SHGs in India using quantitative analysis to know the well performing and poor performing SHGs. The study determined the variables which effectively discriminated the performing and non-performing groups using three quantitative techniques. Discriminate functional analysis was used to discriminate between the groups. The principle component analysis and factor analysis were used to reduce the dimensionality of multivariate data. The above methodology was tested and is statistically significantly in 44 SHGs in the state of Karnataka and recommended that a similar methodology could be used in studies in all the developing countries of the world.

In a study by SINGH *et al.* (2007), it is revealed by using correlation analysis that the individual and the group characteristics had positive and significant relationships with their group performance. In addition, the study also mentions that timely action on training, support, and services has a critical role in their functioning. Performance of SHGs differs depending on the influence of structural and functional variables on the group members, and it was found that financial assistance obtained, frequency of group meetings, supportive environment, group processes, group stability, conformity to group norms, and critical issues of group meetings vary significantly with the level of overall performance (SARADA *et al.*, 2008). On the other hand, satisfaction with the supportive environment significantly contributed for the variation in performance among all the variables selected under the particular study, this indicates that satisfaction with the functioning of the supporting institution plays an imperative role in the work of the SHGs.

There are several factors, such as freedom of participation, motivation, decision-making, group communication, leadership, trust, group homogeneity, and empathy, that play an important role in indicating the effectiveness that brings about group cohesion and better performance (PURNIMA and REDDY, 2007). Furthermore, the research also emphasises that certain indicators are of high relevance for SHG group cohesion. The efficient isolation and control of these indicators influences the changes in performance and productivity of the group considerably. Other study findings (HARE, 1976; NIXON II, 1979; COLE, 1987) also indicate that group participation, chore function, maintenance function, interpersonal trust, and group cohesiveness have a significant relationship with the functioning of SHGs and hence they should function in proper manner for effective and proper functioning of SHGs. In a study on performance of SHGs in Karnataka, NARAYANASWAMY *et al.* (2007) analysed about 50 SHGs and inferred that the SHGs attained medium-level performances and that their performances could be improved by conducting more need-based training programmes and also through market linkages for IGAs taken by the groups. Their findings reveal that transparency in the functioning of the group contributes significantly to the variation in the performances of the groups, and that other factors such as functional linkage, conflict management, and communication between the members are also important factors influencing the performances of the groups. The study by KERR and KAUFMAN (1994) stated that face-to-face communication enhances the likelihood of the individual members to cooperate and, in turn, strengthens solidarity in the group and results in better group functioning. Another study supporting to it, was conducted by the Consultative Group to Assist the Poor (CGAP) in India on sustainability of SHGs. While conducting the study, it analysed the nine SHG models to assess the potentials of the SHG movement (CGAP, 2007). The study reveals that performance depends on their management, systems of operation, membership criteria, freedom of participation, and transparency in administration, record keeping, and social and community action. BARDHAN and DABAS (2007), while studying microfinance initiatives through SHGs, reported that the people in rural India belong to different castes and have different occupations with different socio-economic status and much diversity in their existence; indeed the criteria of group formation results in considerably better functioning of the SHGs. The better performance of the group can be attained by compulsory attendance of the members in the regular meetings. Furthermore, it is also inferred that a higher cost in acquiring the credit increases the value of the credit, increases the responsibility of repayment and the accountability to the groups. Furthermore, the research emphasises that transparency in group activities is a must to maintain the mutual trust between the members and for better functioning of the group. In another study by Jones (2004), while explaining wealth-based trust, it was stated that inequality in the distribution of benefits to the members reduces the trust. However, reduced trust reduces the cooperation in the group and, in turn, hinders the performance, thus indicating the positive relationship between trust and the performance of the groups.

One more study was conducted by the government in Kerala, India, on a comparative study of SHGs organised and promoted by NGOs and a government NGO (*Kudumbasree*) in Kerala. Multistage simple random sampling was used to select 40 SHGs monitored by NGOs and 40 SHGs from the *Kudumbasree* side; a total of 80 SHGs were used as samples for the study (GOVERNMENT OF KERALA, 2004). The detailed socio-economic study found that though there is not much significant difference between NGO SHGs and *Kudumbasree*, the comparative performance of *Kudumbasree* is better than NGO-sponsored SHGs with respect to functioning and empowerment, indicating that the government-managed model is better than other models. The researcher emphasised that this type of study needs to be conducted also in other states, so that the models that are performing better can be given priority over other models and implemented further.

2.2.2. Collective action in Self-Help Groups

The cooperatives were established in India mainly to avoid exploitation of the rural poor and provide them with neighbourhood credit for agricultural production activities along with thrift savings by the members for their emergency needs. But later, the cooperative philosophy of self-help through mutual help – trust that was mostly on paper – had not been successful in previous experiences of cooperative societies, but it is now seeing success in cases of SHGs in India (DWARAKINATH, 1996). SHGs not only benefit the individual women and women's groups but also help their families and communities as a whole through their collective action and solidarity, which are the governing mechanisms of SHGs (SARADA *et al.*, 2008). "Action taken by a group either directly or on its behalf through an organization in pursuit of members' perceived shared interest"[13] and collectivisation implies

13 (Marshall, 1998) http://www.ifpri.org/Themes/gender/Presentation/CAframework.ppt and http://www.capri.cgiar.org/Training/07Feb05_Intro-RMD.ppt.

cohesion of the group (MURUGAN and DHARMALINGAM, 2000). Cohesion enables the members of the group to perceive common interests and act collectively (collective action). The study on the structure of several SHGs showed that the SHGs are largely homogenous with respect to their members' socio-economic backgrounds. This explicitly contributes to freedom of participation, group cohesiveness, and solidarity of the members and, in turn, for the performance of the group (KUMARAN, 1997). An added parallel study to support this emphasises group size, purpose of group formation, homogeneity of group members, terms of office bearers, frequency of meetings, and guiding and operational principles as keys for the success of SHGs (ROUL, 1996b). The study by OSTROM *et al.* on the behaviour of variables within the collective action of the institution revealed that successful collective action in the institution depends on how it behaves with the variables like group homogeneity, free-riding, and self-commitment (OSTROM *et al.,* 1994). In a similar study, OSLON (1965) explained that as group size increased, the probability of achieving the extent of non-optimality increases, and posited that group size also has a significant impact on the collective action of the group.

On the other hand, another study by SIMANOWITZ *et al.* claims that implementation of the SHG programme have missed some of the poorest of the poor due to social and economic factors like caste affiliation, not having a fixed location, migration during lean seasons, and also due to intrinsic biases (SIMANOWITZ *et al.,*1999). This overlooked poorest of the poor who are socially marginalised are difficult to reach and motivate to join. They must be the priority target of the SHGs, who are failed to reach by most of the previous programmes, but can be covered under the SHG net with little extra effort through the same SHG model.

ROSCAs are a classic example of a traditional type of mutual aid or solidarity association and provide an intriguing context to understand collective action. A study on the performance of ROSCA groups (VAN BASTELAER, 2000) emphasised that group size, group homogeneity, communication, and trust between the members have been shown as being important elements of collective action that positively influence the repayment status. Studies by AGARWAL and OSTROM on collective action and the shape of the production function fitted to the structural variables with the collective action related to organising the governance of common resources and institutional sustainability (AGARWAL, 2002; OSTROM, 2001) have identified more than 30 variables that influence collective action through their core relationship and interactions. It is also mentioned that the list is not an exhaustive set of all structural variables that affect collective action and, thereby, it still keeps open the possibility for the entry of other variables into the study of collective action. HARDIN (1976) was one of the first to argue the concept using the help of production function. Furthermore, many scientists have done studies along this line and an extensive analysis is done using different types of production functions like monotonically increasing, linear and non-linear production function relating to individuals with respect to collective action (MARWELL and OLIVER, 1993). The study infers that group heterogeneity is one such variable that may be both a positive and negative determinant of collective action of the group; it can be a challenge or opportunity for the individuals in the group to perform better through a diverse arrangement of rules and norms facilitating greater collective action (DIETZ *et al.*, 2003). The researcher says that several theoretical models have explored the relationship between heterogeneity, collective action, and performance of institutions, and that the heterogeneity does not pre-ordain failures in collective action (POTEETE and OSTROM, 2004). A study on different aspects influencing the collective action in maintenance of irrigation tanks found that heterogeneity of a group with respect to inequality in wealth had a U-shaped relationship with collective action, indicating that the association of these variables with collective action is not straightforward (BALASUBRAMANIAN and SELVARAJ, 2003). Several studies have shown that structural variables like the heterogeneity of a group (HARDIN, 1982), group size, and other factors affect the collective action and, in turn, the performance of the group as all forms of group heterogeneity are not harmful for collective action, indicating group heterogeneity is good in some aspects for better performance of the group and hinders the performance of the group sometimes. Hence in particular to each of the institutions, it is necessary to study the effect of these structural variables on collective action.

In an empirical study (FADIGA and FADIGA STEWART, 2004) on collective action and informal financial institutions of Rotating and Savings Credit Associations (ROSCAs) in Senegal, the focus was on how these ROSCAs were able to overcome the collective action dilemma by maintaining institutional performance and remaining sustainable over time. The study results revealed that monitoring and sanctioning mechanisms in ROSCA have minimised the screening cost for new borrowers. Also, reputations and self-selection of members helped the institution to reduce adverse selection and the moral hazard problem for the association. High rates of interaction, proximity, and effective mechanism such as first-, second-, and third-party enforcement make it easier for mutual monitoring among members and minimises the temptation to default. Social capital such as social norms, networks for relationships, and trust are the important factors that explain how these institutions have been able to remain sustainable and successful. Similar to enforcement mechanism in ROSCA, in the Indian SHGs all the members commit themselves for the loan amount taken by the group, which in turn fortifies the peer group, binding the group members for loan repayment. The study by FUDENBERG and MASKIN (1986) states that when all the members in a group have self-enforced (voluntary) firm commitments to participation in group activities, it eliminates the free-rider problem by following the grim trigger strategy. It means elimination of the one who fails to cooperate in the group when all the members are self-committed.

Despite significant studies in the field, many questions about the importance, influence, and interaction of structural variables with collective action remain unanswered, as the list of variables differs (AGARWAL, 2001). There is little consensus on factors associated with successful collective action (POTEETE and OSTROM, 2003). This keeps open to take up further studies in this direction Remarks on literature reviewed

Based on numerous reviews of research studies, it is clear that microcredit has the ability to eradicate poverty within the social system. In the present context, there are a number of national and international agencies, NGOs, banks, and governments supporting the microcredit concept through SHGs as a means to eradicate poverty all over the world. Based on the methodology followed in past study reviews, it is clear that some studies have focussed on theoretical frameworks like studying the microfinance models in China. On the other hand, some studies have been conducted quantitatively, like the performance of ROSCA, which is studied using log-linear regression considering the variables under study; also, the cooperation and sustainability in ROSCA is studied with respect to group size and group heterogeneity. The current study on the performance of different microcredit delivery models of SHGs in India can definitely contribute to the current research need in this field considering not only financial indicator but also other important indicator for performance like structural variables influencing collective action. The study by SINGH *et al.* (2007) and PURNIMA and REDDY (2007) used correlation analysis to study the degree of relationships between the factors and performance of SHGs and tries to take a similar analysis as in the present study to analyse the relationship between the variables under study and the performance of SHGs under three microcredit models.

In addition the study by RENUKARYA (2004) was related to the performance of SHGs in Karnataka and used quantitative techniques like factor analysis, principle component analysis, and discriminate analysis in studying the performance. The study by RENUKARYA was on selected SHGs, irrespective of the microcredit models, whereas the present study focuses on comparing the factors influencing the performance of SHGs under three microcredit delivery models; this was not undertaken in any of the earlier studies. Moreover, earlier studies on SHGs did not attempt to study collective action, which is included in the present study. Thus, based on the several study reviews mentioned, the methodological approach followed, and the conclusions drawn, the multivariate approach is appropriate for studying the first objective of identifying and comparing the factors influencing the performance of these three microcredit models of SHGs.

Furthermore, a key lesson learnt based on the reviews of collective action is that it is a complex linkage among the variables at different levels, which together affect the collective action and performance of institutions. As scientists say, conducting empirical research on collective action is extremely challenging (OSTROM, 2007) and it is difficult to analyse the entire set of variables and their interaction in a single study (CAMERER, 2003). Hence conducting research with a few important potential variables that have a strong causal relationship is recommended (AGARWAL, 2002; GIBSON, WILLIAMS and OSTROM, 2005; HAYES and OSTROM, 2005) by several researcher. In recent years, microcredit delivery through SHGs is emerging as an alternative mechanism to meet the credit needs of the poor through thrift. This puts forth the need to study the structural and functional characteristics (variables) with respect to their influence on a group's collective action between the three microcredit models. However, the study on group size regarding collective action between the microcredit models of SHGs may not be meaningful since the size of the group is almost the same in all the SHGs under the three models. However, the study on collective action in SHGs can be preceded by selecting two or three important structural variables other than group size for the present empirical study.

Chapter 3 Methodology

"The poor need opportunity, not charity"

- PROF. MUHAMMED YUNUS

For any researcher to fulfil his research objectives, a sound research methodology with appropriate tools of analysis is essential to draw a meaningful inference from the research study and for generalisation of the findings. Hence, this chapter deals with the salient features of the study, sampling technique followed, nature and sources of data used, and the analytical tools and techniques adopted to accomplish the objectives of the research study. This chapter also includes details on the socio-economic profiles of the sample respondents in different models of SHGs.

3.1. Salient features of the study area

India is the seventh largest country in the world and occupies much of the South Asian subcontinent with diverse geography, ranging from snow-capped mountains, desert landscapes, rainforests, hills, and plateaus (FEDERAL RESEARCH DIVISION REPORT, 2004). It is comprised of 28 states and 7 Union Territories. According to the GOVERNMENT OF KARNATAKA (2004), the Indian population was estimated to be 1,065,070,607 with an annual average growth rate of 2 per cent, which amounts to about 17 per cent of the world's population, second in size after China; 72 per cent of India's population reside in rural areas and the population density is about 324 persons per square kilometre.[14] Each of the states has their own ethnicity and language. As per the Indian census lists, there are about 114 languages, and among them 22 are widely used (GOVERNMENT OF INDIA, 2007). There are many programmes that are commonly implemented in all the states by the central government, with SHG banking microfinance being one of the most important. Keeping in mind the objectives of the study, multistage simple random sampling was adopted in selecting the study area and respondents. In this diverse country, based on the availability of time, resources, and communication compatibility of the student

14 http://www.iloveindia.com/population-of-india/index.html.

researcher with the respondents, Karnataka state was purposively selected for the study.

Karnataka is the eighth largest state in India, with an area of 191,791 sq. km and a population of 528,505,620 million. It is predominantly a rural and agrarian state. The northern latitude is between 11.5° and 19.0° and the eastern longitude between 74° and 78° in the southern plateau.[15] It has 27 districts, about 76 per cent of its population lives in rural areas, while about 71 per cent of its workforce is engaged in agricultural and allied activities, which generate 49 per cent of the state income from agriculture crops (GOVERNMENT OF KARNATAKA, 2004). Karnataka accounts for 59 per cent of the country's coffee production and 47 per cent of the country's *ragi* production. It is one of the pioneering states in the microfinance movement of the country. It is among the top three states in the country in terms of credit linkage through SHGs. Based on the NABARD Report (NABARD, 2009), it has about 455,746 SHGs, of which 411,916 SHGs were credit-linked for bank loans at the end of 2008. The model-wise share of SHG microcredit delivery models in Karnataka is depicted in Figure 7. It indicates that Model-III has the highest share, 38 per cent, followed by Model-I and Model-II, with equal shares of about 31 per cent each in the total credit linkage, indicating that all three models are competing equally in reaching the poor.

Fig 7. Model-wise share in delivery of microfinance (%) in Karnataka

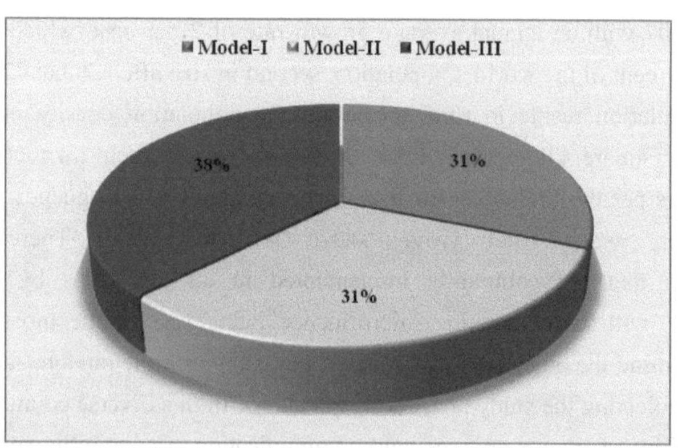

Source: NABARD, 2009.

15 http://karnatakaonline.in/Profile/Data/.

In Karnataka, among the 27 districts in the state, the Davanagere district is purposively selected based on secondary data of the three microcredit models and also considering the criteria's similar number of SHGs in the districts. Figure 8 depicts the study area.

Fig 8. Location of the study area[16]

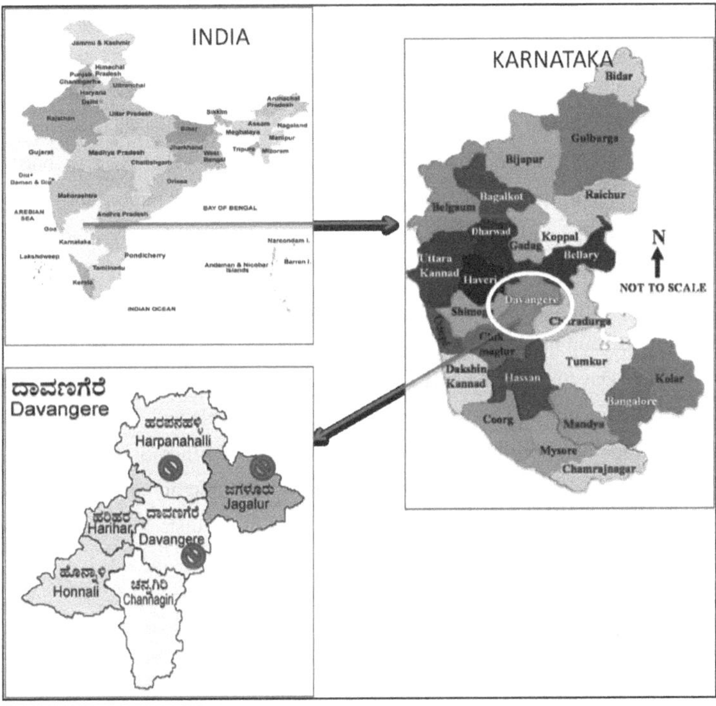

The Davanagere district is located in the central part of Karnataka state with six *taluks,* which together having a geographical area of 0.597 million hectare. The coordinates for this district are 14°27' N latitude to 75°55' E longitude. The district is predominantly agrarian with no major and medium-sized industries. The total population of the district is 1,790,952 with rural and urban population of 1,247,954

16 http://images.google.com/images and http://www.zpdavangere.kar.nic.in/pics/taluk_map.jpg.

(69.68%) and 542,998 (30.32%) respectively, indicating the rural population is prevailing in the district (GOVERNMENT OF KARNATAKA, 2008). The literacy is on par with the average Indian literacy rate for males (76.4%) and females (58%); the average literacy rate of the district is 67.4 per cent. Microfinance through SHGs has been in vogue in the district for the past several years. The institutional credit framework in the district has met 50 to 60 per cent of the total rural credits needed and the rest is being met by informal systems. Hence, the establishment of linkages between banks and SHGs under three different microcredit models is intended to solve some of the problems encountered by banks in extending the credit to the rural poor without any security. There are 19 NGOs operating in the district to organise rural people into SHGs and bank linkage (Annexure 1). The Women and Child Development Department is playing an active role in the formation and linkage of *Sthree Shakti* groups and there are about nine banks that are keenly involved in the promotion and linkage of SHGs in the district. The total number of SHGs in existence in the district is about 15,343 and 12,455 groups are credit-linked under three different microcredit models (NABARD, 2009).

In the Davanagere district, out of six *taluks*, three *taluks* – namely Harapanahalli, Jagalur and Davanagere (Fig. 8) – were selected randomly for study, considering their variability in demographic features. Further SHGs were selected from these three *taluks* and studied with respect to the microcredit delivery models and irrespective of *taluks*. The demographic features of the district and selected *taluks* are presented in Table 2.

Table 2. Selected statistics of selected taluks *in Davanagere district*

Particulars	Davanagere Tq	Jagalur Tq	Harapanahalli Tq	Davanagere District (All 6 Tqs)
Geographical area (sq. km)	994.10	955.27	1,430.24	5,975.97
Number of inhabited villages	153	140	80	810
Population				
Rural	46,198	26,638	40,516	232,869
Urban	71,437	2,857	7,233	104,615
Total Population	602,523	158,883	268,793	1,790,952
Rural	238,000 (39.50)	144,139 (90.72)	226,886 (84.41)	1,247,954 (69.68)
Urban	364,523 (60.50)	14,744 (9.28)	41,907 (15.59)	542,998 (30.32)
Male	309,642 (51.39)	80,954 (50.95)	137,608 (51.19)	917,705 (51.24)
Female	292,881 (48.61)	77,929 (49.05)	131,185 (48.81)	873,247 (48.76)
Population density / sq. km	644	165	187	333

Note: Number in parentheses indicates percentages *Source: Government of Karnataka, 2008.*

In terms of geographical area, Harapanahalli *taluk* has 1,430 sq. km followed by Davanagere *taluk* with 994 sq. km and Jagalur *taluk* with 955 sq. km. But the number of inhabited villages is greater in Davanagere *taluk* and lowest in Harapanahalli. The number of households is higher in urban areas than in rural area in Davanagere *taluk* and vice versa in other *taluk* (Annexure 2). There is not much variation in the male-to-female ration in each *taluk* when compared with the district average. Whereas comparing the rural to urban population shows considerable differences between *taluks:* the Harapanahalli *taluk* has 84.41 per cent rural and 15.59 per cent urban population; Davanagere has 39.50 per cent rural and 60.50 per cent urban population; the Jagalur *taluk* has 90.72 per cent rural and just 9.28 per cent urban population, indicating Jagalur has mostly all rural population (Annexure 3). The literacy rate in the district reflects the Indian average, with a higher literacy rate in the urban population. But the male-to-female literacy rate (%) shows considerable differences, irrespective of rural and urban areas (Annexure 4). However, it is clearer from district working profile data on agriculturist and agricultural labour (Annexure 5) that most of the agriculturists are male and most of the agricultural labourers are female, which shows women do not have ownership of property. It is also emphasised by other studies (MEENA and INTODIA, 1994) that there are no equal rights between men and women regarding property, though it is permitted by Indian legislation. But in work participation, women account for one-third of the labour force involved in agriculture and livestock production (ANITA KUMARI, 2002). The limited availability of access to resources by women in the study area is also expressed by other researchers (BHARATHI, 2005). They emphasised that women empowerment through SHGs is helping women to give access to many of the resources that were inaccessible to them earlier.

3.2. Sampling framework

In the study area, multistage random sampling was adopted to select the sample SHGs and respondents from all three microcredit delivery models. In the first stage, one SHG is selected randomly to collect data from each model in each *taluk* and, thus, a total of three SHGs per *taluk;* in total, data were collected from nine SHGs in the study area. In the next stage, data was collected by randomly selecting 10 members from each selected SHG (Annexure 6). On the whole, it corresponds to 30 sample respondents (SHG members) for each model and thus forms a total of 90 respondents from all three models in the study area. The sampling number and framework was made based on the research review (JAIN and KUHAWALA, 2004) of Self-Help Group studies.

3.3. Sources of data used

The required data relevant to the study was elicited mainly from SHG members as the primary source of data using structured comprehensive questionnaires and collected by personal interview method. A separate semi-structured questionnaire was used to collect detailed information from both SHG members (Annexure 9) and SHGs

(Annexure 10) and covered the following aspects: (i) General information about the family, detailed socio-economic information including family members, average income, occupation etc.; (ii) information regarding SHG membership, its working dynamics, operational indicators, thrift and loan disbursement indicators. The views gathered from respondents through open-end questions were used while discussing the results. The questionnaire for SHG had details like (i) socio-economic information of all the group members; (ii) organisational information about SHGs, covering details of membership, capital resources of the group, group functioning, purpose of loan, record maintenance, etc.; relevant details were gathered.

The required secondary data for the study was collected from government offices, NGOs, banks, and from other institutions. The sources are quoted clearly wherever used in the thesis.

3.4. Variables used in the study and their measurement

3.4.1. Independent variables

In the present study several variables are used in studying the research objectives. These variables are defined below to precisely explain their measurement in the study.

1. **Age:** It refers to the chronological age of the respondents in completed years at the time of the investigation. The respondents are further categorised into three age groups (Table 3) based on the review from MANGASRI (1999) to study the socio-economic profile of the groups. The Age of the members in completed number of years from their Date of Birth is considered in real statistics in the later part of analysis.

Table 3. Categorisation of age

Categories	**Age (in Years)**
Young	Below 35
Middle	36–55
Old	56 and above

2. **Education:** It refers to number of years of formal schooling successfully completed by the respondents. Education of the respondents was quantified

by using the procedure followed by USHARANI (1999). The respondents were grouped into five different categories based on level of education attained (Table 4).

Table 4. Categorisation of education

Categories	Education
Illiterate	Don't know how to read and write
Primary school	1–7
High School	8–10
PUC	College
Degree Holder	University education

3. **Marital status:** Marital status of the respondents was noted by asking the respondents and they were classified based on AICRP-HE study into married, unmarried, widows, or divorced (AICRP, 2001).
4. **Type of family:** The respondents are categorised into two different categories – namely nuclear and joint families – and classification is based on review from SANKANAGOUDAR (1991). Nuclear family represents family with one couple and unmarried children. The joint family means more than a couple and married children living together.
5. **Family size:** The family size is operationally defined based on the number of members residing in the family (Table 5). Classification is supported by HOSAMANI (1993) study review.

Table 5. Categorisation of family size

Family Size	Size
Small	Up to four members
Medium	4–6 members
Large	7 members or more

6. **Occupation:** Occupation refers to the major occupation followed by the Self-Help Group member (respondent). It is categorised based on Government of Kerala study on SHG (GOVERNMENT OF KERALA, 2004) as agriculture,

agricultural labourer, housewife, non-agricultural labourer, small business, pottery, and other, based on the major work profiles of the study area.

7. **Annual income:** It was measured by considering the total income of the family from all the sources; respondents were categorised according to the classification suggested by department of revenue, Government of Karnataka, as indicated below in Table 6 (GOVERNMENT OF KARNATAKA, 1993).

Table 6. Categorisation of annual income

Income group	Annual Income (INR)
Low Income	Up to 11,500
Medium Income	11,500–30,000
High Income	Above 30,000

8. **Caste:** The respondents' information on caste was taken so as to learn which one they belong to; the nominal categorisation is done as Schedule Caste and Schedule Tribe (SC/ST), Other Backward Caste (OBC) and General. The procedure was adopted by MANOHAR *et al.* (1981) for the study on women. The religion is also considered to which they belongs to. The nominal data on Hindu, Muslim, Christian, Jain, and others prevalent in the study area is collected.
9. **Age of SHG:** The age of the group in years is considered from data collected from the time of establishment of the group.
10. **Number of members in SHG:** It is the total number of members existing in the group, which will always be less than 20 as per the SHG rule. The average number of members per SHG under each model is also studied by taking the average of the total number of members in the SHGs under each model.
11. **Nature of SHG:** The information regarding the basis for formation of SHGs is collected from respondents. Different types of SHGs consider different factors, like SHGs formed with members of a similar Age, SHGs with Members from same caste, SHGs with members from similar occupations, or SHGs formed with members from the same location (KARUNA *et al.*, 2006).
12. **Purpose for joining the SHG:** The SHG members are directly asked about their reason for joining the group; it can be for financial security, enhancing

social status, increasing social participation, increasing family business, or any other purpose.

13. **Motivation to become SHG member:** The member respondents were asked a question about who motivated them to become members with options like neighbours, friends, SHG members, and officials of bank/government/NGO, relatives, or any others.
14. **Attending meetings:** The information on members attending the meetings was collected from the respondents and grouped as attending meetings always, sometimes, rarely, or never.
15. **Freedom of participation:** The data on freedom of members in the group participation is collected and is scaled as very actively, actively, seldom, or never. A similar scaling was followed in another study on Self-Help Groups in Karnataka (KARUNA *et al.*, 2006).
16. **Cost involved in acquiring the credit:** The members' expenditures towards acquiring the credit through SHGs was collected and compared with cost of acquiring other sources of credit. It is scaled as least expensive, reasonably expensive, moderately expensive, or most expensive in acquiring the credit.
17. **Risk involved:** The members' response on risk involved in SHGs and in acquiring the credit through SHGs is collected under five categories in the order of least risk, less risk, some risk, more risk, or most risk according to the members.
18. **Transparency in activities:** The respondents' data on the transparency in SHG activities necessary for good functioning was collected under four grade scales in the order of always, sometimes, rarely, or never. The same grade scale was followed by SRIVASTAVA in a study on anti-poverty programmes (SRIVASTAVA, 2002).
19. **Trust of other members:** The data on level of trust of the members for other members of the group was collected and is the base philosophy of SHG formation. Level of trust is scaled as very good, always, sometime, very bad, or never.
20. **Communication of the members:** Good communication is a must for the better functioning of the group. The response of the SHG members on communication between the members within the group is gathered by directly

asking the question of whether communication was very good, always, sometime, very bad, or never.

21. **Decision taken in SHGs:** The decision-making in SHGs was studied from different aspects like: arrive at a consensus after discussing the matter in the SHG; decision taken by majority after discussing the matter in the SHG; leaders and committee members, as per norms from authority or any other. This identifies the decision-making power in the group; Government of Kerala also adopted similar procedure (GOVERNMENT OF KERALA, 2004) in its study.
22. **Record maintenance:** The record keeping in SHG is studied by collecting data from members under six rank scales. The rank is recorded like marginal, below average, average, above average, complete and up-to-date, or virtually no errors. The record maintenance ranking scale is adopted from the CGAP and NABARD study on SHGs (CGAP, 2007) and the ranking details are explained in the questionnaire (Annexure 9).
23. **Subgroups in SHG:** The group members are asked for opinion of yes or no for existence of any subgroups in the SHG that can influence the group; the same is used in the study (GOVERNMENT OF KERALA, 2004).
24. **Satisfaction about the institution:** The respondents were asked yes or no about the question of satisfaction with the workings of their SHG institution, which is essential for the long-term existence of the group.
25. **Knowledge of SHG linkage:** The question asked through the survey was: Do members have knowledge about SHG linkage to bank/government agency/NGO under the three microcredit models? Either yes or no answers were given or the same dichotomous data is used in the analysis.
26. **Selection of office bearers of SHG:** The respondents were asked about the selection of office bearers for the group. During selection, were they selected through election or through consensus?
27. **Savings amount/person/week:** This concerns the individual member contribution to the group thrift amount, which is collected from all the members' regularly in weekly meetings and deposited in the bank.

28. **Total individual savings:** It refers to the total deposit of the individual member through their weekly equal thrift contribution in the group, starting with the establishment of the group.
29. **Loan amount:** This is the amount of credit received by each individual member in the group from their savings and/or also from the bank, with the group responsible for repaying the amount, along with interest.
30. **Subsidy amount:** This is the non repaid amount given to SHGs by government agency/banks or other institutions. This is given to encourage the SHG members to engage in income-generating activities along with savings and thrift activities in SHGs to help them in achieve economic empowerment.
31. **Loan for IGA:** The question was asked through the survey about the purpose of loans taken by members in the group and if they were for income-generating activities (IGA) or not with yes or no type; the data was used in studying loan repayment.
32. **Credit taken is more than thrift amount:** If the SHG member has taken a loan amount that is more than their individual savings in the bank through SHG, then it is considered one of the indicators of proper group functioning and group binding of the members for repayment of a larger loan amount.
33. **Available duration for repayment:** This is the time that is available for the SHG members to repay the loan taken by them from the group.
34. **Members' backgrounds:** The background information of members in the group is collected during the survey to study the homogeneity of members; it is grouped under five scales as in Table 7.

Table 7. Categorisation of members' backgrounds

Members' backgrounds	Scale
All members are from similar backgrounds	1
Most of the members have similar backgrounds	2
At least half of the members have similar backgrounds	3
Few of them have similar backgrounds	4
All are from different backgrounds	5

The above data explained financial variables like individual members savings amount/week, total individual savings, loan amount, subsidy amount; data collected in terms of Indian Rupees (INR) and the same values are used in the analysis.

3.4.2. Dependent variables

In the study, data on a few variables were collected by SHG members and are used as dependent variables in measuring the performance of SHGs and for collective action study objectives at SHG member level. They are described below.

1. **Repayment status:** The respondents were asked about status of repayment of the loan taken in the group. The response was collected in four rank scales: fully paid, regularly paying, irregularly paying, or not started paying. The scaling is adopted from the Kerala government study with slight modifications for fitting the data on repayment status in the study area (GOVERNMENT OF KERALA, 2004). This variable has multinomial-dependent data and the same is used to study the economic performance of the group.
2. **Overall group functioning:** The question was asked through the survey to the members about the overall group functioning, which is considered as a social performance indicator of the group. The response of the members was collected using categorical scales, such as the overall group functioning is: exceptional, above average, average, below average, or poor. The details of the scale are explained in the questionnaire (Annexure 9) and the scaling is adopted from the CGAP and NABARD study on SHGs (CGAP, 2007).
3. **Group cohesion:** The group members are interviewed by asking questions on group cohesion to elicit the collective functioning (collective action in the group) of the group. The members are availed to answer the question under four ordered ranking scales like: below average, average, above average, or outstanding group cohesion, and the same data collected is used in studying the influence of structural variables on the collective action of the SHGs. The details of the scale are explained in (Annexure 9) and the scaling is adopted from the CGAP and NABARD (CGAP, 2007) study on SHGs, with a slight adaptation that is appropriate to the study.

3.5. Analytical tools and techniques used

The suitable statistical tools and techniques employed in the study are detailed below.

3.5.1. Measure of central tendency

Simple statistical tools like frequencies and percentages were used to study the socio-economic profiles of the respondents.

3.5.2. Factor analysis

Factor analysis was mainly employed to identify representative variables from much larger sets of variables for use in subsequent multivariate analyses. The purpose was to retain the few important variables of a large numbers of variables out of the collected dataset. This helps in simplifying the number of variables required for subsequent analysis. It is a multivariate technique used to define the underlying structure in a large data matrix, and in the present study it was used for studying the performance of SHGs. Factor analysis by principal component analysis method can accommodate a large number of variables and reduce the information to a convenient size. The inter-relationship among a set of many inter-related variables were examined and represented in terms of a few underlying factors or dimensions that explain the correlations among a set of variables. Only factors with Eigen values of more than one and based on latent root criterion were considered for the study (HAIR *et al.*, 2005). The purpose behind latent root criterion is that any individual factor should account for the variance of at least a single variable if it is to be retained for interpretation, each variable contributing a value of one to the total Eigen value. The Eigen values are used for establishing a cut-off when the numbers of variables are between 20 and 50; the present study also has a similar number of variables. Only the factors having latent roots or Eigen values greater than one are considered significant and all other factors with latent root less than one are considered insignificant and are disregarded. It assumes that the observed (measured) variables are linear combinations of some underlying source variables (or factors or dimensions). Factor analysis exploits this correspondence to arrive at conclusions about the dimensions (HARMAN, 1968).

Factor loadings provide the correlation between the variable and the underlying dimension. The rotated sum of squares of the factor loadings explains the extracts of the factors in the order of their importance and explains the amount of variance. The product of the corresponding factor loadings can provide the correlation between any two variables.

The factor analysis model in matrix form can be summarised as follows,

$$X\ (n \times 1) = A\ (n \times m) \times F\ (m \times 1) \qquad \ldots\ldots\ldots\ldots\ldots\ldots\ (1)$$

Where,

X = matrix of variables

A = matrix of factor loadings (a_{ij})

F = matrix of dimensions

a_{ij} = net correlation between j^{th} dimension and i^{th} observed variable

n = number of variables

m = number of dimensions

The maximum number of factors possible is equal to the number of variables. However, a small number of factors by themselves may be sufficient for retaining most of the information on the original variables. The researcher RENUKARYA (2004) followed the same technique in his study.

3.5.3. Multinomial Logistic Regression

The multinomial logistic (MNL) regression is a standard method of estimating multi-category dependent variables. An important feature of the multinomial logistic model is that it estimates *j-1* models, where *j* is the number of levels of the outcome variable. The differentiation of quantitative effect of an explanatory variable among different categories of dependent variables is inherent in the multinomial logistic model (MAHAPATRA and KANT, 2005) and hence there is no need to use interactive dummy variables in our case of four different categories of repayment status, which is a dependent variable. The method of restricting the sum of the coefficients to zero was adopted for explanatory variables, which are mutually exclusive and have exhaustive properties of binary (dummy) category (LONG, 1997). The MNL regression is non-linear in nature and the model is developed based on the selected explanatory variables, hence the bias in the parameter estimation due to simultaneous use of many variables in the same equation is avoided (ALDRICH and NELSON, 1984).

The MNL regression model for our study with 'j' categories of dependent variables can be expressed as,

$$ln\left[\frac{p(category_i)}{p(category_j)}\right] = \beta_{io} + \sum_{k=1}^{k=7} \beta_{ik} X_k + \mu \ldots\ldots(2)$$

where,

k = number of independent variables,

j = 4 (fully paid, regularly paid, irregularly paid, not yet started paying),

i^{th} category = fully paid, regularly paid, irregularly paid, and j^{th} category = not yet started paying. There are j categories of dependent variable with j^{th} category as a baseline category or reference category and for baseline category the coefficients are assumes to be zero (NORUSIS, 1999).

X_1 to X_7 are the explanatory variables used in the model defined below.

X_1= age of the members

X_2= number of family members in member's family

X_3= age of SHG

X_4= amount of savings in SHG/person

X_5= loan amount taken/ person

X_6= knowledge of SHG linkage to bank/NGO/ government agency

X_7= satisfaction about the workings of supporting institution

The estimated coefficients ($\beta_0, \beta_1, \beta_2, \ldots, \beta_n$) measure the changes in the ratios of the probabilities termed as odds ratio. The parameter estimates are for the comparison group relative to the reference group and the standard interpretation of the multinomial logit is that for a unit change in the predictor variable, the logit of outcome m relative to the reference group is expected to change by its respective parameter estimate (which is in log-odds units) when all other variables in the model are held constant.[17] The interactive dummy variables for explanatory variables were

17 http://www.ats.ucla.edu/stat/spss/output/mlogit.htm.

not included in this model due to sample-size limitation. The significance[18] is tested using likelihood ratio test[19] (LR test), which is the global test for the impact of one predictor on the dependent variable in general. The Nagalkerke pseudo R-square[20] is used to see that the model fits. The analysis is done using the SPSS 16 software package. In the study, due to sample size limitation, many of the results were not precise enough to recapitulate. Hence, the results are supported by correlation analysis.

3.5.4. Correlation analysis

The correlation coefficient analysis was carried out mainly to assess the degree and direction of the relationship between the variables using Karl Pearson's product correlation method. In the present study, correlation analysis helps to study the nature and degree of the relationship between repayment status and the variables under study.

$$r = \frac{\Sigma (X_i - \bar{X})(Y_i - \bar{Y})}{\sqrt{\Sigma (X_i - \bar{X})^2 (Y_i - \bar{Y})^2}} \quad \text{....... (3)}$$

where,

r = simple correlation coefficient

X = independent variable

Y = dependent variable

$\bar{X}$ = mean of X

---

18 Alpha value was fixed to 10 per cent to test the significance level in the current study.

19 The null hypothesis is that all "*j-1*" coefficients associated with a particular predictor are simultaneously zero. In other words, the global test for the variable X_k tests the null hypothesis that $\beta_{1k} = \beta_{2k} = \ldots = \beta_{(j-1)k} = 0$. That is, X_k has no effect on any of the "*j-1*" logits. The test is a chi-square test based on the difference in chi-square statistics between the full model, with all predictors, and the reduced model, with all predictors except X_k. The test has "*j-1*" degrees of freedom; if it is significant, then X_k has a significant impact on the endogenous variable.

20 Logistic regression does not have an equivalent to the R-square as found in OLS regression, but there are three R-square values obtained, in that Cox and Snell R^2 measures have limitations in model fitting and cannot have a maximum 1 value, but Nagelkerke had a range from 0 to 1 with a modification based on the improvement in the -2LL value and the statistics not exactly means what R-square means in OLS, hence called as Pseudo R-square.

$\bar{Y}$ = mean of Y

n = number of observations

The test of the significance of the result is calculated by comparing with a table value at *n-2* degrees of freedom. Based on past research studies of BHARATHI, NARAYANASWAMY *et al.* and SINGH *et al.,* the present analytical method is adopted (BHARATHI, 2005; SINGH *et al.*, 2007; NARAYANASWAMY *et al.*, 2007). The analysis was done using SPSS 16 software.

3.5.5. Categorical regression

Categorical regression is one type of regression used to describe the relationship between a response variable and a set of predictors. This meta analysis method is developed to quantify the categorical data for assigning numerical values to the categories and an optimal linear regression equation elicited by transformed variables. It is the standard approach when data includes simultaneously nominal, ordinal, and numerical variables. The procedure quantifies categorical variables so that the quantifications reflect characteristics of the original categories. The procedure treats quantified categorical variables in the same way as numerical variables. Using non-linear transformations allows variables to be analysed at a variety of levels to find the best-fitting model. It regresses the response on the categorical predictor values and, consequently, one coefficient is estimated for each variable. For categorical variables, the values are arbitrary and different coding yields different coefficients. The estimated coefficients reflect how changes in the predictors affect the response. The prediction of the response is possible for any combination of predictor values. The R^2 statistic represents how much of the variance in the response is explained by the weighted combination of predictors and used as a measure of how well the regression model fits to the present research data.

The standardised coefficients indicate whether the predicted response increases or decreases when the predictor increases if all other predictors are constant. The category coding determines the meaning of change in a predictor. The value of the coefficient reflects the amount of change in the predicted preference ranking. In addition to the regression coefficients, Pratt's measure of relative importance – i.e., greater individual importance relative to other variable importance corresponds to predictors that are crucial to the regression (PRATT, 1987) – helps in interpreting predictor contributions to the regression. F-test statistic is used in the analysis to see the significance of the variable in the model.

The specifications of the variables used in categorical regression to study the social performance of the models are explained below.

$$Y = \beta_0 + \sum_{i=1}^{12} \beta_i X_i + \mu \ldots\ldots(3)$$

where,

Y= overall group functioning (dependent variable)

β_0 = intercept (only under unstandardised coefficients)

X_1 = nature of SHG

X_2 = purpose for joining the SHG

X_3 = motivation to become SHG member

X_4 = attending meetings

X_5 = freedom of participation

X_6 = transparency in SHG activities

X_7 = trust in other members

X_8 = communication in SHG

X_9 = decisions taken in the SHG

X_{10}= risk involved

X_{11}= cost involved in acquiring the credit

X_{12} = record maintenance

μ = error term

The categorical regression is done for the study using SPSS 16 software package.

3.5.6. Curve-estimation technique

The curve estimation is a simple procedure used to estimate the relationship between the dependent variable(s) and the independent variable when the relationship is not necessarily linear. It is done using the SPSS software package. The software produces regression statistics and fits the curve for 11 different models: linear, logarithmic, inverse, quadratic, cubic, power, compound, S-curve, logistic, growth, and exponential models. Furthermore, based on their relatively good fit for models where a single dependent variable is predicted by a single independent variable, the best model is considered for the study (NORUSIS, 2004). The selected model is used in the study to analyse the influence of selected structural variables, like age of the SHGs, homogeneity of the group, and freedom of participation of the members with the collective action under the three different microcredit delivery models.

In this particular study for the structural variables under study, collective action had a better fit with cubic and quadratic functions and is presented in the results; their general form is presented below.

Quadratic model: $Y = \beta_0 + \beta_1 X + \beta_2 X^2$ .... (1)

Cubic model: $Y = \beta_0 + \beta_0 X + \beta_1 X^2 + \beta_2 X^3$ .... (2)

β = regression coefficients

Y = dependent variable (collective functioning)

X = independent variable under study

The R-square obtained is interpreted as the amount of variance in the dependent variable explained by the model. F-test statistic gives the overall significance of the model (DANIEL and WOOD, 1999).

3.6. Profile of the selected Self-Help Groups under study

The present study is done by collecting primary data from the SHG members of the randomly selected SHGs considering the sampling criteria. The details of the selected SHGs for the study are presented in Table 8. Furthermore, the results are presented under three microcredit models and studied irrespective of the *taluk* and but the selected SHG as a whole to meet the objective of the study.

3.7. Socio-economic profile of the sample SHG members

The socio-economic profile indicates the livelihood status of the respondents. Hence, it necessitates studying the socio-economic information of the respondents before getting into the study. The socio-economic characteristics such as age, education, and marital status, type of family, family size, occupation, religion, caste, and annual income of the sample respondents are presented under the three models of SHGs (Table 9) and discussed below.

Table 8. Details of the SHGs selected for study

Name of the *Taluk*	Name of the SHG	Year started	Number of members
Davanagere (Tq)			
Model-I	Sri Vanitha Mahila SHG	2005	20
Model-II	Sri Shakti Renuka Mahila SHG	2001	15
Model-III	Sri Valmiki Mahila SHG	2007	20
Jagalur (Tq)			
Model-I	Sri Maileshwara SHG	2003	13
Model-II	Sri Laxmi SHG	2003	13
Model-III	Sri Halaswamy Mahila SHG	2007	16
Harapanahalli (Tq)			
Model-I	Sri Sharada SHG	2003	15
Model-II	Sri Choudeshwari SHG	2003	16
Model-III	Sri Kollambika SHG	2003	15

Source: Own compilation, 2009

The age of the respondents are categorised under three groups: young, medium, and old. More than half of the respondents were middle aged in all three models, and about 20 per cent in Model-II and 33.33 per cent in models I and III belonged to the young age group. Of the few remaining people, about 10 per cent in Model-I and 13.33 per cent in Model-III were older than 56 and came under old age group. Interestingly, none of the respondents were from the old age group in Model-III. The results are in line with the results of the study done by RANGI *et al.* (2002). The desire to try innovative ideas and take risks trying to improve living standards with the help of SHGs might be the reason for the predominance of younger respondents.

The educational levels of the sample members in all three models show that more than 60 per cent of the members are illiterate. Among the literate, about 20 per cent, 26.67 per cent, and 13.33 per cent have studied up to primary school in models I, II, and III respectively, followed by members with high school education of 2 per cent in both models I and II, and 4 per cent in Model-III. Only a meagre 1 per cent of respondents received pre-university (3.33%) and university education (3.33%) in Model-I, whereas none of the respondents received pre-university and university education in models II and III. The results are supported by PUHAZHENDI and JAYARAM (1999). The situation might have occurred due to the low financial position of the family, poor education facilities, schools being located in faraway places, and most importantly, the negligence by elders in educating girls. However, few respondents have been educated up to pre-university and college level and it might be because of the growing awareness of the importance of education in the family.

It is clear from the table that most of the respondents were married: 80 per cent, 86.67 per cent, and 76.67 per cent in models I, II, and III respectively. Hence, only a very small percentage of SHG members were unmarried in Model-I (13.33%) and Model-II (3.33%) and no members are unmarried in Model-III. The main reason for a lower percentage of unmarried members in SHGs may be that, in the Indian social system, women have to leave the village and join their husbands once they get married. As SHG is a long-term activity, leaving the group either due to marriage or any other reason would hamper the group activities. This could be the reason in the group for having mostly married members. The remaining percentage of women was from the widow and divorced categories. The models II and III have 10 per cent and 20 per cent widows ,respectively, and only 3.33 per cent in Model-I. The number of divorced women is negligible, with 3.33 per cent in both models I and III, and in Model-II none of the respondents were divorced. However, it is reassuring to see that the weakest among the weaker category of women, namely the widows and divorced, were also taking part in SHGs, thereby gradually becoming self-reliant and stable in leading their lives.

Nuclear families were the dominant family type in all three models. In Model-I 70 per cent of the respondents were from nuclear families; the remaining 30 per cent belonged to joint families; whereas in Model-II about 96.67 per cent belonged to a nuclear family and the remaining 3.33 per cent to a joint family. In Model-III all the respondents were from nuclear families. The results concur with the findings of HEMALATHA PRASAD (1997) and PRASAD (1998). The predominance of nuclear families might be due to the fact that most of the respondents are from poor families with marginal land or landless labourers, and lack of physical and financial assets made them choose nuclear families to reduce their responsibilities.

The information on the size of families clearly says that among the respondents, about 80 per cent in Model-I and 60 per cent in both models II and III were from medium-size families. Model-I has an equal percentage of respondents (10%) from small and large families. Similarly, Model-III has 20 per cent respondents from both small and large families. However, Model-II has 23.33 per cent from small families and 16.67 per cent from large families. The results are in line with the findings of KUMARAN (1997) and MAHAPATRA *et al.* (1997) and they have found that this might be due to their awareness regarding the increased cost of living and difficulties in the maintenance of a big family and lack of family support in small families. Hence, they might have found that it is beneficial to have medium-size families to lead a better and comfortable life.

The occupation of the respondents is an important factor in determining the economic condition of the SHG members. In all three models, most of the respondents were working as agricultural labourers, and the next largest majority were involved in agriculture as an occupation in Model-II (56.67%), Model-I (36.67%), and Model-III (20%). Only Model-I has 6.67 per cent of respondents working as a housewife, and none in models II and III, which indicates it is necessary for women's earning to be agricultural labourer to meet the financial requirements of the family. The respondents working in other occupations were few, indicating the scope for women to enter into many of the non-agricultural and small-business activities – either individually or through their group in the village – to improve their financial status was limited. Similar results were recorded by KUMARAN (1997) and PRASAD (1998) – that the majority of women were engaged as agricultural labourers due to lack of physical and material resources.

The socio-economic study also focussed on the respondents' religions and caste profiles to show the distribution of members in the group. The data elucidates that more than 85 per cent of the respondents belong to the Hindu religion in all three models, with 96.67 per cent in models I and II, and 86.67 per cent in Model-III. The few remaining respondents belonged to a Muslim religion, and no respondents were from other religions like Christianity or Jainism, though the related population prevails in the study area.

The study reveals that in Model-I, the different castes of the sample respondents are equally represented in the groups – SC/ST (33.33%), OBC (30%), and General (36.67%) – whereas Model-II has more than half of the respondents from the OBC caste and the remaining 46.67 per cent from SC/ST. However, in Model-III, over three-fourths (86.67%) of the respondents belong to SC/ST and just 13.33 per cent to the OBC group, but interestingly in Model-II and Model-III, none of the respondents were from the General caste. The results are supported by the SUDHARANI (2002) study, in which it was found that SHGs covered most of the SC/ST population. On the other hand, still a majority of the poor are from SC/ST group, which is the main target group of SHGs.

The annual income of the family reveals that more than half of the respondents in all three models fall under the 11,500–30,000 INR income category with 63.33 per cent in Model-I and 50 per cent in models II and III. About 40 per cent in Model-II, 43.33 per cent in Model-III, and only 26.67 per cent in Model-I fall in the below 11,500 INR income category. However, in all three models, 10 per cent or fewer of the respondents were from the above 30,000 INR category. This emphasises that the SHGs target, that is, the poorest of the poor and those on the poverty line, were covered in all three models.

The average number of members per SHG revealed that there is not much difference in the number of members per SHG between the three models. In a nutshell, the socio-economic features show that there are no big differences in the members' profiles across all levels of the three models. The results conform with the findings from a comparative study of SHGs from government departments and NGOs in Kerala state (GOVERNMENT OF KERALA, 2004). The findings from their detailed socio-economic study about members has found that there is no significant difference between the socio-economic status of members in NGO-monitored SHGs and *Kudumbasree*-monitored SHGs.

Table 9. Socio-economic profile of the sample members (n=30, N=90)[21]

Particulars	Model-I	Model-II	Model-III
Age			
Young (below 35 years)	10 (33.33)	6 (20.00)	10 (33.33)
Middle (36–55 years)	17 (56.67)	20 (66.67)	20 (66.67)
Old (56 years and above)	3 (10.00)	4 (13.33)	-
Education			
Illiterate	20 (66.67)	20 (66.67)	22 (73.33)
Primary school	6 (20.00)	8 (26.67)	4 (13.33)
High school	2 (6.67)	2 (6.67)	4 (13.33)
PUC	1 (3.33)	-	-
Degree holders	1 (3.33)	-	-
Marital status			
Unmarried	4 (13.33)	1 (3.33)	-
Married	24 (80.00)	26 (86.67)	23 (76.67)
Widows	1 (3.33)	3 (10.00)	6 (20.00)
Divorced	1 (3.33)	-	1 (3.33)
Type of family			
Nuclear	21 (70.00)	29 (96.67)	30 (100.00)
Joint	9 (30.00)	1 (3.33)	-
Family size			
Small (up to 4 members)	3 (10.00)	7 (23.33)	6 (20.00)
Medium (4–6 members)	24 (80.00)	18 (60.00)	18 (60.00)
Large (7 and above)	3 (10.00)	5 (16.67)	6 (20.00)
Occupation			
Agriculture	11 (36.67)	17 (56.67)	6 (20.00)
Agriculture labour	16 (53.33)	12 (40.00)	22 (73.33)
Housewife	2 (6.67)	-	-
Non-agri labour	-	-	1 (3.33)
Small business	-	-	-
Pottery	-	1 (3.33)	-
Other	1 (3.33)	-	1 (3.33)
Religion			
Hindu	29 (96.67)	29 (96.67)	26 (86.67)
Muslim	1 (3.33)	1 (3.33)	4 (13.33)
Caste			
SC/ST	10 (33.33)	14 (46.67)	26 (86.67)
OBC	9 (30.00))	16 (53.33)	4 (13.33)
General	11 (36.67)	-	-
Annual income (INR)			
Up to 11,500	8 (26.67)	12 (40.00)	13 (43.33)
11,500–30,000	19 (63.33)	15 (50.00)	15 (50.00)
Above 30,000	3 (10.00)	3 (10.00)	2 (6.67)
Average members/SHG	16	16	17

Note: Figures in parentheses indicate percentage of the respective total. *Source: Own compilation, 2009*

21 "n" indicates the total sub-sample from each model and "N" indicates the total sample under study from all the models, which is sum of number in each row.

Chapter 4 Results and Discussion

This study in the Davanagere district of Karnataka deals with the performance of different microcredit delivery models at the SHG level and the influence of structural variables on collective action of SHGs under three models. The empirical results and discussion of the study are presented in six different sections. The first section provides important factors that are significantly different between the SHGs in the three models. The second, third, and fourth sections focus on the results of correlation analysis, MNL regression, and categorical regression, respectively, to study factors influencing the performance of SHGs under the three models. The fifth section attempts to study the influence of structural variables on collective action in the context of three microcredit models of SHGs. In the sixth section, which includes the overall results of the study, hypotheses are discussed and, based on the study, important variables influencing the performance of SHGs were mapped.

4.1. Factor influencing the performance of SHG microcredit delivery models

During the study, information was collected from the respondents that covered many of the aspects. Further, the most important variables influencing SHGs in the three models are identified using factor analysis. Before doing factor analysis, the variables are tested for significance by using the *Kruskal-Wallis* test to know which variables significantly differ between the three models (Table 10). The results indicate that the personnel profile variables like caste, marital status, main occupation, and type of family significantly differ between the models. The group characteristics such as the nature of the SHG, age of the SHG, terms of office bearers, number of members in the SHG, meeting attendance rates, dropouts from the SHG, action taken against an SHG member for non-involvement in SHG activity, satisfaction of SHG member with the workings of the supporting institution, training programmes conducted for SHG members, and overall group functioning also have shown significant differences between the models. The variables related to savings and credit, like total savings amount of individual in the SHG, loan amount taken per person, interest rate paid for the loan amount, cost involved in acquiring the credit compared to other sources of credit and risk involved in it, the purpose of loan being taken, steps taken for delay in loan repayment by the members, punishment for delayed loan repayment, credit taken that equals more than the savings amount of SHG members, available instalments, and duration of loan repayments have revealed significant differences between the SHGs of the three models under study. Thus, the above variables create significant differences between the models and are used further in the current study. It clearly indicates that though the three models are focussed on the same population with the same objective, they differ in many of the factors, which in turn can influence the performance of the SHGs under the three models. Significant statistical differences in the models for all the variables mentioned in Table 10 were found at the 5-per cent level.

Table 10. Test of significance for variables under study between SHG models

Variable	Chi-square	Sig.
Caste	12.687	.002
Marital status	7.001	.030
Main occupation	7.632	.022
Type of family	7.367	.025
Nature of SHG	6.457	.040
Age of SHG	28.886	.000
Term of office bearers	28.972	.000
Number of members in SHG	8.603	.014
Attending meetings	20.597	.000
Dropouts	25.395	.000
Action taken against SHG member for non-involvement	19.391	.000
Satisfaction about the workings of supporting institution	11.270	.004
Training programmes conducted	26.061	.000
Overall rating of group functioning	45.036	.000
Total individual savings amount in SHG	8.897	.012
Loan amount/person	63.440	.000
Interest rate on loan	43.310	.000
Subsidy amount/person	24.244	.000
Cost involved in acquiring the credit	12.757	.002
Risk involved in acquiring the credit	8.661	.013
Purpose of loan	6.984	.030
Steps taken for delay in loan repayment	8.692	.013
Punishment decision for delayed loan repayment	6.345	.042
Credit taken more than thrift	8.063	.018
Available instalments for loan repayment	24.250	.000
Available duration of loan repayments	15.964	.000

Note: All variables in table are significant at 5-per cent level. *Source: Own compilation, 2009*

Table 11. Total variance explained by factor analysis

Component	**Model-1**			**Model-2**			**Model-3**		
	Rotation Sums of Squared Loadings (Eigen values)			Rotation Sums of Squared Loadings (Eigen values)			Rotation Sums of Squared Loadings (Eigen values)		
	Eigen values	% of variance	Cumulative %	Eigen values	% of variance	Cumulative %	Eigen values	% of variance	Cumulative %
1	22.718	29.125	29.125	16.226	20.033	20.033	14.378	17.534	17.534
2	11.149	14.294	43.419	14.284	17.635	37.668	13.116	15.995	33.529
3	6.245	8.006	51.425	6.603	8.152	45.819	12.168	13.961	47.489

Extraction Method: Principal component extraction method.

Source: Own compilation, 2009

The factor analysis is used to create a subset of variables from a larger set, based on the original variables that have the highest correlation with the principal component factors and also by handling the multicollinearity between the variables. The results of the factor analysis are presented in Table 11 and Table 12.

The most important components and their relative explanatory power as expressed by their Eigen values, considering the latent root criterion, are presented in Table 11. It also explains the total amount of variance explained by each component to the total variation in the set of variables under the factor matrix. It is clear from the results that all the models have three components explaining their extracted factor loadings. The extracted components explain the factor loadings, wherein Model-I explains about 51.42 per cent of total variance extracted by the factor solutions, followed by Model-III with 47.48 per cent, and 45.81 per cent in Model-II.

In Model-I, the first component explains 29.12 per cent variance, followed by the second and third components, with 14.29 per cent and 8 per cent, respectively. In the case of Model-II, 20.03 per cent and 17.63 per cent of variance was explained by the first and second components and 8.15 per cent by the third component, whereas in Model-III, the first component explained 17.53 per cent variation, followed by the second and third components with 15.99 per cent and 13.96 per cent respectively.

In Table 12, the rotated component matrix loadings for identified factors are given and the values represent the loadings of variables on their respective component. This helps in identification of the variables that have large loadings on the same component. This also explains how well each variable is explained by the component. It can be seen from the table that in Model-I, the first component is explained by the loading of several variables that act in different directions. The age of the SHG, membership fees, credit amount taken above person's savings level, cost involved in acquiring the credit, subsidy amount per person, and discussion of social problems have significantly higher loadings with positive signs and are grouped for having same pattern of loading. The other variables, like number of members in the SHG, savings amount per person per week, total individual savings amount in SHG, loan amount/person, interest rate on loan, available instalments, and duration of loan repayments all have higher factor loadings with negative signs indicating these variables move in opposing patterns to the previous group. In the case of the second component, training programmes conducted and interest rate on deposits are the two variables with negative signs explaining considerable factor loadings, whereas attending meetings and equal opportunity to become office bearer are the two variables with opposing patterns, with positive signs explaining the third component.

It is apparent from Model-II that the variables like age of the SHG, number of members in the SHG, savings amount per person per week, total individual savings amount in the SHG, and loan amount per person load significantly on the first component, with positive signs and other variables like cost involved in acquiring the credit, available instalments for loan repayments, and interest rate on deposits having negative signs moving in the opposite direction with higher loadings on the component. In the second component, subsidy amount per person and credit amount taken above a person's savings have positive signs with higher loadings and move in the same pattern, whereas attending meetings moves in the opposite direction with a higher negative loading. Only the variable training programme had positive sign loads on the third component.

Model-III has detained variables like age of the SHG, number of members in the SHG, and terms of the office bearer with a significant positive sign load on component one, whereas membership fees, savings amount per person per week with a negative sign load significantly on component one and move in opposing patterns. However, the interest rate on deposits and credit amount taken above a person's savings both have opposing signs and load significantly on the second component. The variables such as attending meetings and caste are significantly positive, with a higher factor loading on the third component.

The extracted factor loadings (Table 12) show that the variables loading on each component vary significantly both in sign and value from one model to other. The variables that are under the first, second, and third components of Model-I are not necessarily under the first, second, and third components of the other models and vice versa, emphasising that the direction and magnitude of variance of each variable in explaining the factor loadings of the components varies from one model to the other and, furthermore, that these variables are used in studying the performance of SHGs under three models. Similar results were observed by RENUKARYA (2004) in his study on performance of SHGs and mentioned that many factors with different factor loadings influence the performance of SHGs under study.

Table 12. Rotated components matrix explaining factor loadings of each variable on extracted component

Variables	Model-I	Model-II	Model-III
Component: 1			
Age of SHG	0.918	0.942	0.898
Number of members in SHG	-0.865	0.803	0.942
Membership fees	0.990	-	-0.979
Savings amount / person/week	-0.990	0.915	-0.898
Total individual savings amount in SHG	-0.941	0.915	-
Credit amount taken above savings	0.990	-	-
Cost involved in acquiring the credit	0.990	-0.927	-
Loan amount/person	-0.990	0.961	-
Interest rate on loan	-0.990	-	-
Subsidy amount/person	0.990	-	-
Available instalments for loan repayment	-0.926	-0.872	-
Available duration of loan repayment	-0.971	-	-
Discussion of social problems	0.921	-	-
Interest rate on deposits	-	-0.927	-
Terms of the office bearer	-	-	0.968
Component: 2			
Training programme conducted	-0.894	-	-
Interest rate on deposits	-0.894	-	-0.920
Subsidy amount/person	-	0.932	-
Attending meetings	-	-0.860	-
Credit amount taken above savings	-	0.845	0.979
Component: 3			
Attending meetings	0.864	-	0.954
Equal opportunity to become office bearer	0.806	-	-
Training programme conducted	-	0.938	-
Caste	-	-	0.875

Source: Own compilation, 2009

4.2. Relationship between economic performance (repayment status) independent variables

The relationship between the repayment status and several other variables is studied by carrying out correlation analysis. The findings revealed that each variable has expressed its relationship differently under the three models – the results are presented in Table 13. It was observed that age of the member was not significantly related with the repayment status in all three models. This implies that the SHG members' loan repayment status is not associated with age. The variable castes had a positive but not significant relationship with the repayment status in Model-I, whereas in Model-II and Model-III there was a positive and significant relationship at the 10-per cent and 5-per cent levels, respectively. The possible reason for this might be their exposure to the social system and awareness about the benefits. The education of the respondents has a positive and significant relationship with repayment status, both in Model-I and Model-II, but in Model-III, the relationship is positive but not significant. However, it is clear that the majority of the respondents were illiterate (Table 9); there was a higher number of educated people in Model-I and Model-II compared to Model-III and, moreover, education brings changes in the attitudes and perceptions of SHG members.

Annual income was found to be positive in all the models and significant in Model-I and Model-II and not significant in Model-III, because with higher income, risk-bearing capacity increases and, in turn, increases repayment by members. Similar results for education and annual income were reported by SINGH *et al.* (2007) in their study indicating that economic empowerment of the group was found to have a positive relationship with education, family occupation, and annual income of the members in the group. The number of people in SHG members' families had a positive but not significant relationship with repayment status. The existence of subgroups within an SHG had a negative relationship with status of repayment in all the models and was found to be significant in Model-II and not significant in Model-I and Model-III. It indicates that the existence of subgroups within an SHG will have a negative effect on repayment status, more so in Model-II compared to the other models. The selection of office bearers of the SHG had a negative relationship in the three models, and it was significant in Model-I and not significant in Model-II and Model-III. This means that selection of office bearers by election was found to not be necessary by the groups due to the group cohesiveness or feeling of equal responsibility by every member of the group. But, a few SHGs are interested in selecting the office bearers in rotation but not doing so, since a change of office bearers involves extra work in the clerical transfer of bank accounts and other documents. Hence, the office bearers are not changed in a few groups to avoid this clerical work. Moreover, they feel there is not much difference in having the same office bearers or in rotating them. Similar findings were reported by the CGAP (2007) study on SHGs in India, mentioning that the same members were re-elected to avoid the problem of changing bank signatories and to make new people familiar with the regular procedure. The knowledge of SHG linkage to these models by SHG members was observed to have a positive relationship in all three models and to be significant in Model-I and Model-III and not significant in Model-II. This implies that the knowledge of the SHG bank linkage by members has a positive influence on repayment status in Model-I and Model-III and was not observed in Model-II. The satisfaction about the workings of supporting institutions expressed by the members is significantly positive in Model-I and significantly negative in Model-II and Model-III, which implies that satisfaction with the workings of supporting institutions has shown to have a significantly positive influence on repayment in Model-I, whereas it did not have a significant relationship in the other two models. The purpose for joining the SHG, age of the SHG, and number of members in the SHG was not found to have a significant relationship with repayment.

It was observed that the total individual savings of members in the SHG had a highly significant, positive relationship with repayment in Model-I and Model-II, whereas in Model-III it was not significantly positive or strongly related with repayment status. The results revealed that the savings amount collected per person per week was highly significant and positive in relationship with repayment in all three models. The strategic opportunity given by SHGs to its members to save along with the credit lending and subsidy in peer group has helped in the realisation of safe savings deposits in SHGs even with the illiterate members. This might be the reasons for the observed behaviour in the savings and repayment relationship. The loan amount was found to have a significantly positive relationship with repayment in Model-I and a negative one in Model-II, and did not have a significantly negative relationship in Model-III. On analysis, the reason for the difference in the relationship was attributed to the purpose for which the loan amount was utilised. In Model-I as loan amount increases, the higher the repayment status will be, since most of the loans were taken for income-generating activities like animal husbandry, which earns income for the members to repay the loan under close supervision of a supporting institution. But in Model-II most of the loans by members were taken to meet their emergency needs like meeting education expenditures of children, for marriages, for hospital expenditures, and less for production activities when close supervision by a supporting institution was lacking. There was a positive and significant relationship between the amount of subsidy given and the loan repayment status in Model-I and Model-III, implying that a subsidy given to the members is encouraging them to repay the loan by tying themselves to incentives given to them and their group. However, in Model-II there is a significantly negative relationship with repayment status. The reason behind this is SHG members are not doing the loan repayment for the credit taken, thinking that the credit amount is a measly amount to the government along with subsidy given. The variables like loan taken for IGA, credit taken is more than the savings amount; the available duration for repayment has a significantly positive influence on repayment status in Model-I and Model-II, except the non-significant positive relationship for credit taken is more than savings amount in Model-III. This implies that peer group pressure coupled with a convenient repayment schedule in terms of number and available instalments for loan repayment might be the reason for the positive relationship between these variables with repayment.

In a nutshell, several social and economic variables have shown different relationship patterns with loan repayment status and, in turn, had an effect on economic performance of SHGs under the three models considered in the study.

4.3. Results of MNL regression on economic performance of micro-credit models

The economic performance of SHGs under three microcredit models was studied at the members' level by considering loan repayment status of members (Fig. 6) as a dependent variable, since the dependent variable had multiple outcomes; it is fitted with multinomial logistic regression, taking into consideration other statistical criteria. The seven independent variables explained in equation (1) were the explanatory variables used in the analysis and the results are presented below. The results presented in Table 14 compare and explain the regression coefficients of each of the explanatory variables for multinomial dependent variables under the three microcredit models. In the dependent variable, having not yet started paying is a reference category; the other three categories are comparison categories explained in reference to it. Hence, in the study three multinomial logit equations were estimated under each microcredit delivery model.

Table 13. Relationship between economic performance (repayment status) and social and economic characteristics

Variables	Correlation coefficient		
	Model-I	Model-II	Model-III
Social indicator			
Age of the member	0.105	0.060	0.306
Caste	0.292	0.536**	0.480*
Education	0.377*	0.363*	0.249
Annual income	0.406*	0.389*	0.232
Number of people in SHG member family	0.237	0.316	0.205
Any subgroups within SHG	-0.170	-0.363*	-0.249
Selection of office bearers of SHG	-0.566*	-0.17	-0.140
Knowledge of SHG linkage to bank/NGO/gov. agency	0.539*	0.214	0.289*
Satisfaction about the workings of supporting institution	0.420*	-0.186	-0.200
Purpose for joining SHG	0.131	0.232	0.327
Age of the SHG	-0.109	-0.080	0.310
Number of members in SHG	0.052	0.240	0.176
Economic indicators			
Total individual savings amount in SHG	0.902**	0.997**	0.898
Savings amount collected/ person/ week	0.924**	0.968**	0.799**
Loan amount	0.866*	-0.440*	-0.116
Subsidy amount	0.980**	-0.799*	0.447*
Loan for IGA	0.559**	0.377*	0.433*
Credit taken is more than thrift amount	0.566*	0.377*	0.158
Available duration for repayment	0.945**	0.500**	0.995*

*Note: * significance at 5-per cent level, ** Significance at 10-per cent level Source: Own compilation, 2009*

Table 14. Parameter estimates of multinomial logistic regression for economic performance of microcredit models

Independent variables	Dependent: Repayment status					
	Model-I		Model-II		Model-III	
	B	Sig.	B	Sig.	B	Sig.
Fully paid / not started						
Intercept	75.472	0.968	40.560	0.991	59.028	0.953
X_1	0.011	0.888	0.246	0.153	-0.076	0.748
X_2	-0.154	0.007	-2.445	0.095	-1.430	0.132
X_3	23.918	0.416	29.995	0.984	25.362	0.984
X_4	20.733	0.047	-0.051	0.989	-2.726	0.956
X_5	0.008	0.061	-0.012	0.982	-0.003	0.127
X_6	0.101	1.000	-4.193	0.396	10.826	0.009
X_7	0.939	0.570	3.448	0.196	0.088	0.976
Regularly paid / not started						
Intercept	-69.246	0.991	2.141	0.998	11.034	0.998
X_1	0.013	0.838	0.137	0.373	-0.187	0.407
X_2	-3.341	0.989	-0.539	0.421	-0.438	0.414
X_3	6.945	0.989	10.923	0.083	8.911	0.083
X_4	6.206	0.989	-0.017	0.975	-1.365	0.978
X_5	0.001	0.813	-0.001	0.986	0.001	0.175
X_6	-14.129	0.991	-10.526	0.024	24.164	0.996
X_7	2.168	0.119	1.577	0.462	-1.181	0.649
Irregularly paid / not started						
Intercept	126.851	0.918	286.923	0.912	-33.132	0.997
X_1	-0.060	0.545	-4.134	0.958	-1.467	0.277
X_2	-0.019	0.781	7.201	0.963	2.719	0.452
X_3	16.711	0.038	97.952	0.093	85.451	0.094
X_4	-19.465	0.052	-0.253	0.757	1.759	0.978
X_5	0.007	0.009	-0.027	0.907	0.002	0.414
X_6	-15.272	0.990	-16.791	0.894	30.123	0.997
X_7	-0.842	0.635	19.362	0.951	-3.790	0.377
Nagelkerke R^2	0.429		0.853		0.868	
–2 Log Likelihood Ratio Test	28.365		57.861		57.330	

Note: Not started paying is reference category *Source: Own compilation, 2009*

(Note: X_1 = Age of the members; X_2 = Number of family members in member's family; X_3 = Age of SHG; X_4 = Amount of savings in SHG/Person; X_5 = Loan amount taken/ person; X_6 = knowledge of SHG linkage to bank/NGO/ government agency; X_7 = satisfaction about the workings of supporting institution.)

Based on the results, the equations for each of the multinomial outcomes for all the three microcredit models are presented below:

Model-I:

$$\ln\left[\frac{p\,(\text{Fully paid})}{p(\text{Not yet started})}\right] = 75.472 + 0.011X_1 - 0.154X_2 + 23.918X_3 + 20.733X_4 + 0.008X_5 + 0.101X_6 + 0.939X_7$$

$$\ln\left[\frac{p\,(\text{Regularly paid})}{p(\text{Not yet started})}\right] = -69.246 + 0.013X_1 - 3.341X_2 + 6.945X_3 + 6.206X_4 + 0.001X_5 - 14.129X_6 + 2.168\,X_7$$

$$\ln\left[\frac{p\,(\text{Irregularly paid})}{p(\text{Not yet started})}\right] = 126.851 - 0.060X_1 - 0.019X_2 + 16.711X_3 - 19.465X_4 + 0.007X_5 - 15.272X_6 - 0.842\,X_7$$

Model-II:

$$\ln\left[\frac{p\,(\text{Fully paid})}{p(\text{Not yet started})}\right] = 40.560 + 0.\,246X_1 - 2.445X_2 + 29.995X_3 - 0.051X_4 - 0.012X_5 - 4.193X_6 + 3.448X_7$$

$$\ln\left[\frac{p\,(\text{Regularly paid})}{p(\text{Not yet started})}\right] = 2.141 + 0.137X_1 - 0.539X_2 + 10.923X_3 - 0.017X_4 - 0.001X_5 - 10.526X_6 + 1.577X_7$$

$$\ln\left[\frac{p\,(\text{Irregularly paid})}{p(\text{Not yet started})}\right] = 286.923 - 4.134X_1 + 7.201X_2 + 97.952X_3 - 0.253X_4 - 0.027X_5 - 16.791X_6 + 19.362X_7$$

Model-III:

$$\ln\left[\frac{p\,(\text{Fully paid})}{p(\text{Not yet started})}\right] = 59.028 - 0.076X_1 - 1.430X_2 + 25.362X_3 - 2.726X_4 - 0.003X_5 + 10.826X_6 + 0.088X_7$$

$$\ln\left[\frac{p\,(\text{Regularly paid})}{p(\text{Not yet started})}\right] = 11.034 - 0.187X_1 - 0.438X_2 + 8.911X_3 - 1.365X_4 + 0.001X_5 + 24.164X_6 - 1.181X_7$$

$$\ln\left[\frac{p\,(\text{Irregularly paid})}{p(\text{Not yet started})}\right] = -33.132 - 1.467X_1 + 2.719X_2 + 85.451X_3 + 1.759X_4 + 0.002X_5 + 30.123X_6 - 3.790X_7$$

In all the above equations, the coefficients of explanatory variables are interpreted as the change in the log-odds of the comparison group to the reference group associated with a unit change in the predictor variable, while other variables are held constant in the model. The negative and positive sign of the coefficients indicates the increase or decrease in the log-odds keeping all other predictors constant. The variables knowledge of SHG linkage to bank/NGO/ government agency (X_6) and satisfaction about the workings of supporting institution (X_7) have dummy variable with yes or no outcomes, hence the outcome no is evaluated at parameter estimate zero.

Fully paid/ not yet started Logit:

The intercept in the estimated MNL regression equation infers the multinomial logit estimate of fully paid category relative to not yet started when the predictor variables in the fitted model are evaluated at zero, which was observed to be positive under the three microcredit models: Model-I (75.472), Model-II (40.560), and Model-III (59.028). In the case of the first predictor, for a unit change in the age of the members (X_1), the log-odds of the respondents in the category of fully paid increases by a factor of 0.011 in Model-I and 0.246 in Model-II, whereas in Model-III, log-odds decrease by 0.076 as it has a negative sign. The variable number of family members in member's family (X_2) has a negative sign for logits in all the microcredit models and it is significant in Model-I and Model-II but insignificant in Model-III. Results explain that an increase in the number of family members by one unit, log-odds of being in a fully paid group relative to reference group decreases by the following factors: Model-I (0.011), Model-II (0.246), and Model-III (0.076). The coefficient of the third variable, age of SHG (X_3) has a positive sign and is insignificant in all three models. One unit change in the age of the SHG had log-odds in favour of fully paid increases by a factor of 23.918 in Model-I, 29.995 in Model-II, and 25.362 in Model-III. The fourth predictor, amount of savings in SHG per person (X_4), is significant in Model-I and not significant in the other two models; log-odds of falling under fully paid category increases by a factor of 20.733 in Model-I and decreases in Model-II by 0.051 and Model-III by 2.726, with one unit change in the amount of savings in SHG per person. The fifth variable, variable loan amount taken per person (X_5), showed a significantly positive sign in Model-I and was not significant and showed a negative sign in Model-II and Model-III. As loan amount taken per person increases by one unit, the log-odds of preferring the fully paid category over the reference category is expected to increase in Model-I (0.008) and decrease in Model-II (0.012) and Model-III (0.003). The coefficient for yes in relative to no regarding knowledge of SHG linkage to Bank/NGO/ Government agency(X_6) is 0.101 unit higher in Model-I, 4.193 unit lower in Model-II and 10.826 unit higher in Model-III for preferring fully paid category over not yet started. In other words, in Model-I and Model-III respondents with knowledge of SHG linkage to bank/NGO/government agency are more likely to be under fully paid category over not yet started category than respondents with no knowledge, but vice versa in Model-II. The coefficient for the variable satisfaction about the workings of supporting institution (X_7) is not significant in all three models and explains that being satisfied with the workings of supporting institution, the probability of observing respondents in the fully paid category compared to not yet started category increases by 0.939 in Model-I, Model-II (3.448), and Model-III (0.088).

Regularly paid/not yet started Logit:

The estimated MNL regression equation for regularly paid category with reference group had a negative intercept for Model-I (69.246), whereas Model-II (2.141) and Model-III (11.034) had positive values. The coefficients of the variable age of the members (X_1) explains that a unit increase in the variable increases the likelihood of respondents being in the regularly paid category in Model-I by a factor of 0.013, in Model-II by 0.137, and in Model-III it decreases by 0.187. The estimated coefficients for number of family members in member's family (X_2) denotes that when number of family members in member's family increases by one unit, the log-odds of a respondent in favour of the regularly paid category decreases by a factor of 3.341, 0.539, and 0.438 in Model-I, Model-II, and Model-III, respectively. The coefficients of the third variable, age of SHG (X_3), has positive signs and results show that with an increase in the age of the SHG by one unit, the higher the likelihood of being in the regularly paid category in all the models; model-wise the values are: Model-I (6.945), Model-II (10.923), and Model-III (8.911). Similar results were observed in a study by MOHAMADOU and LESLIE (2004), which emphasised that defaults were less likely to occur in the groups that have existed from a long time. The variable amount of savings in SHG per person (X_4) increases the log-odds of being in the regularly paid category over reference category by 6.206 in Model-I, whereas it decreases by a factor of 0.017 and 1.365 in Model-II and Model-III, respectively. In the case of the fifth variable, for one unit change in loan amount taken per person (X_5), the log-odds in favour of being included in the regularly paid category increases by 0.001 in both Model-I and Model-III, whereas in Model-II it decreases by a factor of 0.001. The estimates of the sixth variable, yes in relationship to no regarding knowledge of SHG linkage to bank/NGO/government agency (X_6), for preferring regularly paid category over reference category is lower in Model-I and Model-II by 14.129 and 10.526 units, respectively, and higher by 24.164 units in Model-III. The estimates of variable satisfaction about the workings of supporting institution (X_7) were observed to be positive in Model-I and Model-II and negative in Model-III. This means being satisfied about the workings of a supporting institution increases the probability of falling in the regularly paid category with respect to reference category by 2.168 in Model-I and 1.577 in Model-II, whereas probability of falling in the regularly paid category decreases by 1.181 in Model-III.

Irregularly paid/not yet started Logit:

In the results of MNL regression for the third comparison group, it was observed that Model-I (126.851) and Model-II (286.923) have high intercept values with positive signs but Model-III (33.132) has negative values. The coefficient estimates of age of the members (X_1) variable indicates that for a unit change in the variable, the log-odds of the respondents being in the irregularly paid category over the not yet started category decreases in all the models and it decreases by a factor of 0.060 in Model-I, 4.134 in Model-II, and 1.467 in Model-III. The variable number of family members in a member's family (X_2) was observed to have the likelihood of being in the irregularly paid category over the reference category decreases by log-odds value in Model-I (0.019), whereas log-odds increase in favour of irregularly paid category in Model-II (7.201) and Model-III (2.719). In the case of the third predictor, age of SHG (X_3), the results explains that for a unit change in the variable, the log-odds of being in the irregularly paid category over the reference category increases by 16.711 units, 97.952 units, and 85.451 units in Model-I, Model-II and Model-III, respectively. The fourth variable, amount of savings in SHG per person (X_4), is significant in Model-I and not significant in the other two models and the results denote that one unit change in the amount of savings in the SHG per person, the log-odds of being in the irregularly paid category decreases in both Model-I (19.465) and Model-II (0.253), but increases in Model-III (1.759). The loan amount taken per person (X_5) variable was observed to be significant and showed positive signs in Model-I and not to be significant in Model-II and Model-III, which showed negative signs and positive signs, respectively. The estimates explain that as the loan amount taken per person increases by one unit, the log-odds of being in the irregularly paid category over the reference category is expected to increase by a factor of 0.007 units in Model-I, 0.002 units in Model-II, but log-odds decrease by a factor of 0.027 units in Model-III. The variable estimates for yes in relation to no regarding knowledge of SHG linkage to bank/NGO/government agency (X_6) is lower by 15.272 units in Model-I, 16.791 units in Model-II, but 30.123 units higher in Model-III for being in the irregularly paid category over the not yet started category. The satisfaction about the workings of the supporting institution (X_7) variable observed a decrease in the probability of being in the irregularly paid category over the not yet started category by a factor of 0.842 and 3.790 in Model-I and Model-III, respectively; on the other hand, the probability increases by 19.362 units in Model-II for being satisfied about the workings of the supporting institution.

In the above results, regression coefficients of independent variables for each multinomial outcome in the equations are tested for significance by Wald statistic test[22] and the corresponding *p* probability values observed under null hypothesis were also included in Table 14. In OLS regression, R^2 value gives the explanatory power of selected independent variables to the dependent variable. Whereas, the MNL regression does not have an equivalent to the R-square as found in OLS regression. But Nagelkerke's R^2 value presented in the table will explain the goodness of fit of the MNL regression; it also indicates the strength of association of the explanatory variables with the dependent variable. The results revealed that Model-I (0.429) has low Nagelkerke's pseudo R^2 value, indicating frail strength of association compared to good strength of association in Model-II (0.853) and Model-III (0.868). The –2 Log Likelihood Ratio test is a test of significance for the overall model fit and it indicates the chi-square statistics for the overall fit of MNL regression function. The analysis reveals that the MNL regression function is significant at 10 per cent in Model-I with a 28.365 chi-square value, whereas in Model-II and Model-III, overall

22 The null hypothesis tested is that predictor's regression coefficient is zero given that the rest of the predictors are in the model.

fit of MNL regression function is significant at 5 per cent with 57.561 and 57.330 chi-square values, respectively.

In addition to Wald statistics, the results for the Likelihood Ratio (LR)[23] test of the explanatory variables used in the MNL regression are presented in Table 15 as the study was conducted with a limited sample.[24] The likelihood ratio test is used to test the significance of the contribution of each explanatory variable to the overall MNL regression model. The results revealed that in Model-I, the explanatory variables like amount of savings in SHG per Person (X_4), loan amount taken per person (X_5), and satisfaction about the working of supporting institution (X_7) are significant at the 5-per cent level and other predictors are not significant contributors. In Model-II all the predictors except age of SHG (X_3) and satisfaction about the workings of the supporting institution (X_7) are significant at the 5-per cent level and only age of the members at the 10-per cent level. In the case of Model-III, the predictor age of SHG (X_3) is not significant, followed by satisfaction about the workings of the supporting institution (X_7), which is significant at the 10-per cent level, and the rest of the variables are significant at the 5-per cent level in explaining their contributions to the overall MNL regression function. The odds ratio table (Annexure 7) gives the odds ratio associated with each explanatory variable considered in the model. The odds ratio of a coefficient indicates how much the risk of the outcome is falling in the comparison group compared to the risk of outcome falling in the not yet started referent group.

---

23 When the coefficients are large, standard errors get inflated and thereby lowers the Wald statistics leading to Type II errors (MENARD, 2002). Hence for Logit models, where dummy variables are used and coefficients are very large, LR test used to test the difference of models with and without the parameter.

24 The Wald statistics are sensitive to violations of the large sample assumptions of logistic regression. In another way, the LR test is considered more reliable for small samples (AGRESTI, 1996), thus the LR test of individual model parameters is generally preferred.

Table 15. Likelihood test of explanatory variables used in MNL regression

Independent variables	Likelihood Ratio Test Chi-Square		
	Model-I	**Model-II**	**Model-III**
Intercept	0.000	0.000	0.000
Age of the members (X_1)	0.781	10.011**	16.509*
Number of family members in member's family (X_2)	3.412	10.159*	8.587*
Age of SHG (X_3)	0.658	6.037	1.253
Amount of savings in SHG/Person(X_4)	3.897*	7.896*	20.433*
Loan amount taken/person (X_5)	1.082*	11.479*	17.405*
knowledge of SHG linkage to bank/NGO/ Government agency (X_6)	3.157	21.793*	8.871*
satisfaction about the working of supporting institution (X_7)	6.037*	3.263	1.849**

*Note: * significance at 5-per cent level, ** significance at 10-per cent level. Source: Own compilation, 2009*

The higher value of odds ratio for a variable denotes that apart from the variables included in the model there are some other causal variables that cause high probability of being in comparison group relative to the group under reference.

4.4. Results of categorical regression on social performance of microcredit delivery models

In the present study, the social performance of the SHGs under three microcredit delivery models was studied by considering the overall group functioning as a dependent variable indicating the social performance of the SHGs; the findings are presented in Table 16. The dependent variable is categorical in nature and the 12 predictor variables considered in the study are nominal, ordinal, and numeric in nature and the details of the variables are explained in the methodology. Considering the nature of the data under study, categorical regression analysis was done to study the importance of each variable with respect to the dependent variable. The standardised coefficients indicate the change in the response variable with a change in the variable under consideration keeping the other variables constant. The categorical regression standardises the variables, hence the standardised coefficients are presented in the table as these coefficients explain, regardless of the predictor's scale of measurements. The Pratt's values are also presented, which indicate the relative importance of the transformed variables. The results of the analysis are explained below.

The standardised coefficients in the table explain the relationship between the predictor and the response variable (social performance). In the case of the nature of the SHGs (X_1), a one standard deviation increase of the variable in the grouped order yields a 0.517 and 0.278 standard deviation increases in the overall group functioning in Model-I and Model-III respectively, and decreases the standard deviation by 1.280 in Model-II. The predicted response of overall group functioning decreases by a standard deviation of 0.327, 0.552, and 0.016 in Model-I, Model-II, and Model-III, respectively, for one standard deviation change in purpose for joining the SHG (X_2). In the case of the variable motivation to become SHG member (X_3), one standard deviation change explains an increase in the response variable by a standard deviation of 0.632 in Model-I, but a decrease in the response variable by a standard deviation of 0.312 in Model-II and 0.052 in Model-III is observed.

Table 16. Categorical regression results for social performance (overall group functioning as dependent variable)

Predictors	Model-I				Model-II				Model-III			
	Standardised Coefficients				Standardised Coefficients				Standardised Coefficients			
	Beta	Std. Error	Pratt's	Sig.	Beta	Std. Error	Pratt's	Sig.	Beta	Std. Error	Pratt's	Sig.
X_1	0.517	0.126	0.307	0.001*	-1.280	0.222	0.191	0.001*	0.278	0.161	0.047	0.123
X_2	-0.327	0.159	0.042	0.074**	-0.552	0.123	0.110	0.003*	-0.016	0.162	0.002	0.923
X_3	0.632	0.128	0.364	0.000*	-0.312	0.150	0.025	0.081	-0.052	0.150	-0.012	0.946
X_4	0.069	0.161	0.009	0.679	-1.214	0.150	0.808	0.000*	0.195	0.255	-0.043	0.466
X_5	0.316	0.118	0.129	0.028*	0.929	0.208	0.005	0.007*	0.053	0.153	0.004	0.740
X_6	0.050	0.152	-0.002	0.751	-0.206	0.130	-0.004	0.172	0.370	0.208	0.012	0.097
X_7	0.311	0.126	0.146	0.025*	0.813	0.154	0.234	0.003*	0.506	0.130	0.262	0.005*
X_8	0.217	0.123	0.089	0.117	-0.547	0.159	-0.185	0.018*	-1.047	0.284	0.137	0.003*
X_9	-0.036	0.147	-0.013	0.979	-0.458	0.118	0.070	0.008*	-1.028	0.214	0.399	0.000*
X_{10}	0.110	0.121	0.006	0.388	0.654	0.138	0.112	0.003*	0.213	0.129	0.036	0.139
X_{11}	-0.332	0.134	-0.077	0.025*	-0.462	0.180	-0.133	0.040*	-0.477	0.163	0.183	0.019**
X_{12}	0.266	0.161	0.017	0.137	-0.168	0.117	-0.013	0.213	-0.414	0.173	-0.029	0.029*
R^2 value	0.734				0.776				0.697			

*Note: * significance at 5-per cent level, ** significance at 10-per cent level.* *Source: Own compilation, 2009*

(X_1 = Nature of SHG; X_2 = Purpose for joining the SHG; X_3 = Motivation to become SHG member; X_4 = Attending meetings; X_5 = Freedom of participation; X_6 = Transparency in SHG activities; X_7 = Trust in other members; X_8 = Communication in SHG; X_9 = Decisions taken in the SHG; X_{10}= Risk involved; X_{11}= Cost involved in acquiring the credit; X_{12} = Record maintenance.)

The overall group functioning observed an increase in standard deviation in Model-I (0.069) and Model-III (0.195), and a decrease in Model-II (1.214) for a unit standard deviation change in the predictor attending meetings (X_4). The dependent variable increases by a standard deviation of 0.316, 0.929, and 0.053 units in Model-I, Model-II, and Model-III, respectively, for a unit change in the standard deviation in the freedom of participation (X_5). In the case of transparency in SHG activities (X_6), a one standard deviation increase of the variable results in 0.050 and 0.370 standard deviation increases in the overall group functioning in Model-I and Model-III, respectively, and decreases the standard deviation by 0.206 in Model-II. The coefficient of trust in other member (X_7) indicates that a standard deviation change of 0.311 in Model-I, 0.813 in Model-II, and 0.506 in Model-III in the dependent variable was observed for one standard deviation change in the variable. The one standard deviation change in the variable, communication in SHG (X_8) explains a standard deviation increase of 0.217 in Model-I, whereas Model-II and Model-III had standard deviation decreases of 0.547 and 1.047, respectively. The predicted response of overall group functioning decreases by standard deviations of 0.036, 0.458, and 1.028 in Model-I, Model-II, and Model-III, respectively, for one standard deviation change in the variable decisions taken in the SHG (X_9). One standard deviation change in the variable risk involved (X_{10}) increases the standard deviation of the dependent variable by 0.110, 0.654, and 0.213 units in Model-I, Model-II, and Model-III, respectively. The one standard deviation increase in the variable, cost involved in acquiring the credit (X_{11}), explains the decrease in the standard deviation of overall group functioning in Model-I (0.332), Model-II (0.462), and Model-III (0.477).

The results of the analysis for Model-I revealed that, among the 12 explanatory variables under study, the variables nature of SHG (X_1), motivation to become SHG member (X_3), freedom of participation (X_5), trust in other members (X_7), and cost involved in acquiring the credit (X_{11}) are significant at the 5-per cent level and the variable purpose for joining the SHG (X_2) is significant at the 10-per cent level. The standardised coefficients also reflect the importance of predictor and the Pratt's value measures the relative importance of predictor; the results revealed that motivation to become an SHG member, nature of the SHG, trust in other members, and freedom of participation are the important explanatory variables in order in the fitted function under Model-I explaining the social performance.

In Model-II, except for motivation to become an SHG member (X_3), transparency in SHG activities (X_6) and record maintenance (X_{12}), all other variables are significant at the 5-per cent level. The standardised coefficients and the Pratt's value reveal that in Model-II, variables like attending meetings (X_4), trust in other members (X_7), nature of SHG (X_1), risk involved (X_{10}), and purpose for joining the SHG (X_2) are in order of importance in explaining the social performance of the group.

The variables like trust in other members (X_7), communication in SHG (X_8), decisions taken in the SHG (X_9), and record maintenance (X_{12}) are significant at the 5-per cent level, and cost involved in acquiring the credit (X_{11}) is significant at the 10-per cent level; the remaining variables considered are insignificant in Model-III. The most important explanatory variables in the order of importance based on the standardised coefficients and the Pratt's values in influencing the social performance of the group are: decisions taken in the SHG (X_9), trust in other members (X_7), cost involved in acquiring the credit (X_{11}), and communication in SHG (X_8).

The R^2 value in the fitted categorical regression function for considered predictors was 0.734 in Model-I, 0.776 in Model-II, and 0.697 in Model-III. This shows that the variance in social performance in Model-I (74%), Model-II (78%), and in Model-III (70%) is explained by the coefficients of the optimally transformed predictors indicating the overall model fit.

The findings of the above analysis infer that the performance was observed to improve in the SHGs formed based on attributes, in order: age, caste, occupation, and location based. It indicated that groups formed comprising the neighbours will perform better than the groups formed based on other factors in Model-I and Model-III and vice versa in Model-II. Furthermore, in all three models, the groups with the purpose for joining SHGs for financial security have increased social performance, followed by the SHGs formed for other purposes. The motivation to become an SHG member also influences the performance of the group. The highest performance is observed if motivated by neighbours, followed by performance of the SHGs as a motivation to become an SHG member, and then go, in order, from neighbours to other options like friends, SHG members, officials of NGO/bank/government, relatives, or any other in Model-I, but vice versa in Model-II and Model-III. The groups with members attending the meetings always had better performance, followed by the groups where members attending meetings is sometimes, rarely, and never in Model-I and Model-II, and vice versa in Model-III, indicating there is more equal responsibility of members. Decision-making by the group and activeness of the group is more in Model-I and Model-II, compared to Model-III. Supporting the present results, BARDHAN and DABAS (2007) reported that groups can perform better if they ensure compulsory attendance of the members in the regularly held meetings.

The social performance of the groups in all the models was observed to be the highest where member participation is very active, followed by the performance of groups having actively, seldom, and never having freedom of participation. The performance of the group was found to be highest if the transparency in SHG activities is always ensured, followed by reduced performance if transparency in the SHG is sometime or never. The findings are in conformity with the NARAYANASWAMY *et al.* (2007) study stating that transparency in the functioning of SHGs significantly contributes to the variation in the performance of SHGs at the group level. The results reveal that trust in members has a direct impact on social performance, as the trust that changes the overall group functioning also changes in the same manner all the models, indicating social performance of groups will be higher when the trust between members is very good and decreases as trust decreases. Similar results were observed by JONES (2004), who explains how reduced trust reduces the cooperation in the group and, in turn, the performance.

The communication in the SHG also influences directly the overall functioning of the group in Model-I, but inversely in Model-II and Model-III, which may be because of less interaction by the government agency workers and NGO officials with all the members. The results are in line with KERR and KAUFMAN'S (1994) findings that face-to-face communication enhances solidarity in the group and enhances better functioning through good cooperation. The performance in all the models was observed to be more in the SHGs, which take decisions based on the consensus arrived at after discussing the matter in the SHG meeting followed by the groups, which take decisions based on the majority after discussing the matter in the SHG and based on leaders and committee members – as per norms from authorities or any others in the order – indicating that the cooperation and consent of all the members is equally important for the group performance.

In all the models, it was observed that the lesser the risk involved in the group in acquiring the credit, the higher the social performance of groups and vice versa, indicating the risk involved in acquiring the credit through the SHG is also a crucial factor that influences the members' participation and, in turn, the performance of the group. The performance of SHGs was observed to be better in all three models when the cost involved in acquiring the credit was most expensive, compared to the lesser cost in acquiring the credit through SHGs, indicating the increased cost in getting credit forces the members to bind themselves more in the group to do better, thereby increasing the performance. Similar results were reported by BARDHAN and DABAS (2007) in their study on microfinance initiatives through SHGs, revealing that the higher cost in acquiring the credit makes the borrowers in the group understand the value of credit, makes them accountability to the group, and shows them the importance of repayment. In the study area in Model-II and Model-III, the performance of SHGs was observed to be exceptionally good when the record maintenance was better with virtually no errors and minimum record maintenance, followed by lesser performance in SHGs, where records are maintained at marginal level by maintaining only basic records which are being maintained minimally, whereas Model-I had not shown this trend. This result might be because the group members have self-interest in Model-I and have comparatively more trust, belief, and peer pressure within the group, which is positive for the overall group functioning and has no external actors involved in the group activity, unlike the involvement of government workers in Model-II and NGO workers in Model-III.

4.5. Collective action study using structural variables at SHGs in three microcredit delivery models

The collective action of the group depends generally on the nature of the structural variables existing in the group. A study by OSTROM *et al.* revealed that successful collective action in the institution depends on how it behaves with the variables like group homogeneity, free-riding, and self-commitment (OSTROM *et al.*, 1994). Another study by OSLON (1965) argued that group size also has an impact on collective action of the group. In the present study, the collective action of the SHGs under different microcredit delivery models was studied and compared for variables like members' backgrounds (homogeneity of participants), freedom of participation (free-riding), and age of the SHGs (commitment of group over time) while the variable group size is not studied as it is uniform in all the SHGs under the different microcredit models. A similar type of study was done by AGARWAL (2000) and MARWELL and OLIVER (1993). The present study is done using a curve-estimation technique to study collective action behaviour with the selected variables under study and the results are described below. The R^2 value and F-statistic for fitted curve model is presented in Annexure 8. In the analysis, collective functioning marks the collective action of the group and is measured with a four-graded scale explained in Annexure 9, from a lowest of below average collective action, to average, above average and outstanding collective action in the SHGs under study.

4.5.1. Homogeneity of group members and collective action

The collective action in the SHGs is studied with respect to homogeneity of the participants under three microcredit models and the results are presented in Figure 9 for Model-I, Figure 10 for Model-II, and Figure 11 for Model-III. As explained in the methodology, the homogeneity of members was measured with a five-grade scale considering the member's background, one indicates highest homogeneity in the group with all members from similar backgrounds, and five indicate the least homogeneity in the group with all members from different backgrounds. Taking the homogeneity of the group members on the X-axis and collective action on the Y-axis, the curve estimation fitted a third-order functional relationship between the variables and the results for three models and are listed below.

Model-I: $Y = 3.205 - 0.504\,X + 0.117\,X^2 + 0.010\,X^3$

Model-II: $Y = 2.775 + 0.001\,X - 0.057\,X^2 - 0.011\,X^3$

Model-III: $Y = 2.818 + 0.0001\,X - 0.017\,X^2 - 0.010\,X^3$

In Model-I, when the group is homogeneous with all the members from similar backgrounds (Fig. 9), the collective action was observed to be between average and above average; a decrease in group homogeneity of members showed an increasing trend in collective action towards outstanding functioning and crossed the above-average level. This type of behaviour might be because these SHGs are formed by members coming together voluntarily who have a common interest and objective to have better livelihoods and, moreover, they have self-enforced commitments, which last longer. Hence, when members are from different backgrounds, the diversity in the group helped them to come up with better ideas and solutions to have outstanding collective action, as members have self-interest in free and fair discussions about their problems in group meetings. The results are in conformity with MARWELL and OLIVER (1993), who state that homogenous groups contribute zero resources and heterogeneous members give their own contributions, adding greatly to the total benefits and better group functioning. In contrast to the behaviour in Model-I, the collective action of the group in Model-II (Fig. 10) was observed better with the homogeneity of members and is reduced to the below-average level when only half of the members are homogenous, further showing the decreasing trend in collective action as the homogeneity of the group decreases. These SHGs were formed by government workers by mobilising the people from different communities that met government specifications for group formation. After group formation, with less monitoring from the workers, the groups with members of similar backgrounds showed better collective functioning with better peer understanding. The decreasing trend was observed in collective action and SHG activities with members from different backgrounds with less peer binding.

The results were supported with the study findings of BARDHAN and DABAS (2007), namely that people in rural India belong to different castes, occupations, and socio-economic statuses, and hence there should be thinking that homogeneity should be the basis of classification for better performance of SHGs. In the case of Model-III (Fig. 11), the groups have above-average levels of collective action when there is more homogeneity of the group and show a slight declining trend as the homogeneity of the group lowers, but not as much as in Model-II. This might be because the SHGs in Model-III were formed by NGOs and, hence, monitored by them when required to have normal group functioning, thereby creating better understanding between the members and peer capacity-building, which helps the collective action in the groups to stay above average.

4.5.2. Age of the SHGs and collective action

The age of the groups is also one of the structural variables posited to affect the collective action of the group over time, hence the variation in the level of collective action with age of the groups is studied in three models; the results have shown a second-order production function relationship for the variables. The second-order production function was found to best fit two variables under the study by taking the age of the SHG in year units on the X-axis and collective action scales plotted on the Y-axis; the functions are presented in Figure 12 for Model-I, Figure 13 for Model-II, and Figure 14 for Model-III.

Model-I: $Y = 12.900 - 3.250\,X + 0.250\,X^2$

Model-II: $Y = -8.800 + 4.200\,X - 0.400\,X^2$

Model-III: $Y = 1.875 + 0.088\,X + 0.001\,X^2$

Fig 9. Homogeneity of the group members vs. collective action in Model-I

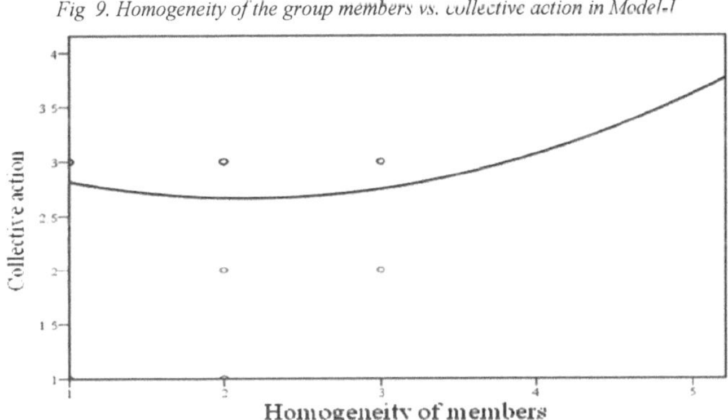

Fig 10. Homogeneity of the group members vs. collective action in Model-II

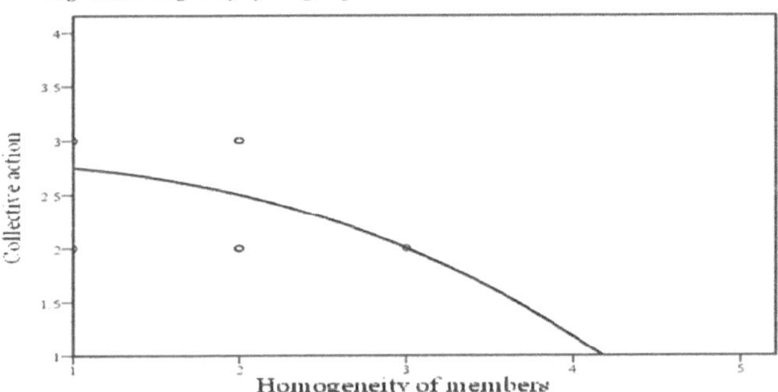

Fig 11. Homogeneity of the group members vs. collective action in Model-III

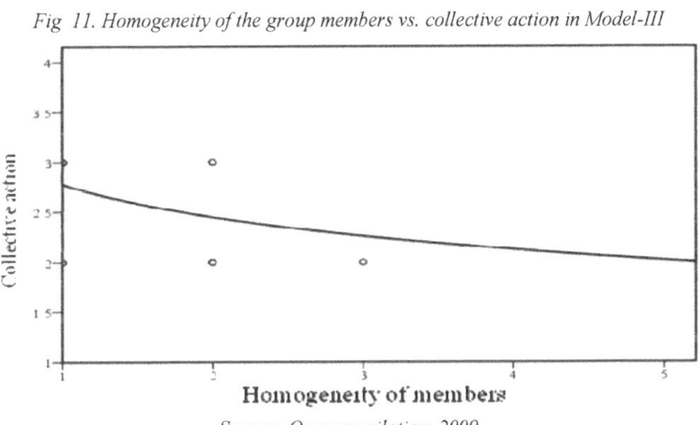

Source: Own compilation, 2009

Fig 12. Age of the SHGs vs. collective action in Model-I

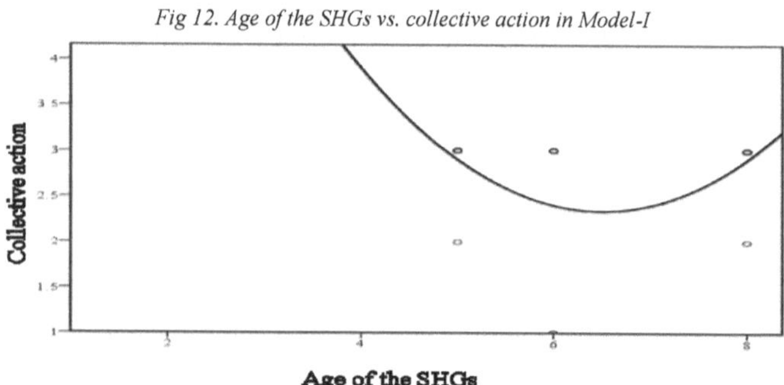

Fig 13. Age of the SHGs vs. collective action in Model-II

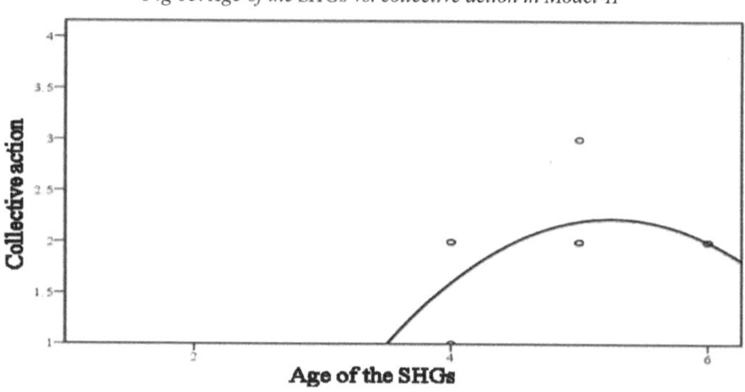

Fig 14. Age of the SHGs vs. collective action in Model-III

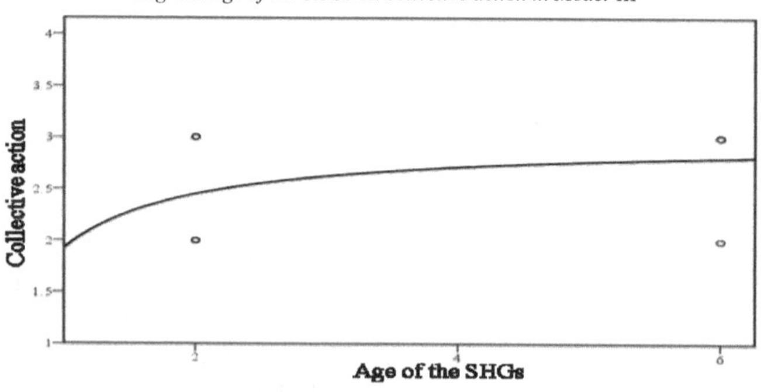

Source: Own compilation, 2009

The second-order production function relationship between age of the groups and collective action for Model-I (Figure 12) reveals that the collective action level in the group was outstanding in the beginning and beyond as the age of the group increases the trend observed to move towards above-average and outstanding level. This indicates that in Model-I, collective action in the group with respect to age of the SHGs was observed always at the average level and above, and never went below the average level. The members have come together with a self-commitment to participate fairly and consistently in the group over time for better collective action, which resulted in good collective functioning with an increase in the age of the SHGs.

In the case of Model-II, the relationship between age of the group and collective action had shown opposite trends – in the beginning period of group formation, the collective action was below the average level; it was later observed at the average level, and further on, as the age of the SHG increases, the collective action by the members in group declines (Fig. 13). It might be because as the government agency brings people together and forms the group, it takes time for the group in the initial days to bond with a close rapport and to have trust, mutual faith, and compatibility to participate freely in group meetings, which observed an increase collective action in the group. Later, collective action of the group was observed to have a downward trend with less monitoring from the government as the peers bonding was sometime not voluntarily, as in Model-I. The pattern of behaviour observed was quite different in Model-III (Fig. 14), though the collective action was at an average level in the initial years of group formation, but with the stronger group binding over time and minimum required support from the NGOs as and when required by SHGs, there was a consistently steady increase in collective action as the group became older.

4.5.3. Freedom of participation and collective action

The freedom of participation of members in the group indicates how the members are involved in all the activities of the group and in taking decisions that contribute towards better group functioning. On the other hand, in the absence of freedom of participation by the members is a sign of a free-rider problem, which affects the collective action of the group. Thus, taking freedom of participation with a four-grade scale like very actively, actively, seldom, and never as an indicator of free-riding in the group, the collective action is studied under three microcredit models. The study found that a third-order functional relationship exists between freedom of participation and collective action, explained below and presented in Figure 15 for Model-I, Figure 16 for Model-II, and Figure 17 for Model-III.

Model-I: $Y = 2.578 + 0.001\,X + 0.012\,X^2 - 0.007\,X^3$

Model-II: $Y = 1.871 + 0.405\,X + 0.002\,X^2 - 0.048\,X^3$

Model-III: $Y = 2.680 - 0.005\,X + 0.002\,X^2 + 0.012\,X^3$

In Model-I, the collective action in the groups was observed between the average and above average levels when all the members had the freedom to participate very actively in all the regular group activities; it shows a slight decline as freedom of participation of members moves towards seldom and never participatory status (Fig. 15). This indicates that in these SHGs, as the participation of members in the group decreases, the overall group functioning is reduced as it becomes difficult for the selected member office bearers to take decisions individually on activities affecting the collective action when members participation is seldom or never in the group. It was observed that no free-rider can exist in these SHGs as most of the decisions are arrived at by consensus and are under close watch by banks officials. A similar opinion was given by FUDENBERG and MASKIN (1986) stating that if players in a group are self-enforced and strongly commit themselves eliminates free-riding by following the grim trigger strategy. Model-II (Fig. 16) depicted that with very active freedom of participation of all members; it results in comparatively better collective action in the group. As freedom of participation of members is reduced, the collective action of the group goes below the average level. This kind of behaviour implies that once the group is formed by a government agency, it facilitates the group members to participate actively in group activities; if all members are involved with interest, then the performance of the group increases without any free-rider and offers positive yields for collective action. But on the other hand, if members are not participating, then office bearers take decisions individually and this provides room for unintentional free-riders. Furthermore, if no members in the group are interested, then government workers lose their interest in the group, in turn reducing the collective action in the group.

Unlike in Model-I and Model-II, the behaviour is quite different in Model-III (Fig. 17). If NGO officials are commonly involved in the situation, the collective action of the group was at an average level. With all members participating very actively in SHG activities and in decision-making processes, the collective action was at an average level after taking into account all the group members considerations, interests, and preferences and balancing them for better group functioning. But when the participation of members is lower, an upward trend in collective action is observed. On analysis it is found to be because, the members participate in the group, but less with respect to decision making, as they are following the guidance of NGO officials to make decisions in many of the SHG's activities. This resulted in better collective action in the group as NGO officials give unbiased and judicious decisions, suggestions and opinions, which are accepted by all and favour outstanding collective action.

Fig 15. Freedom of participation vs. collective action in Model-I

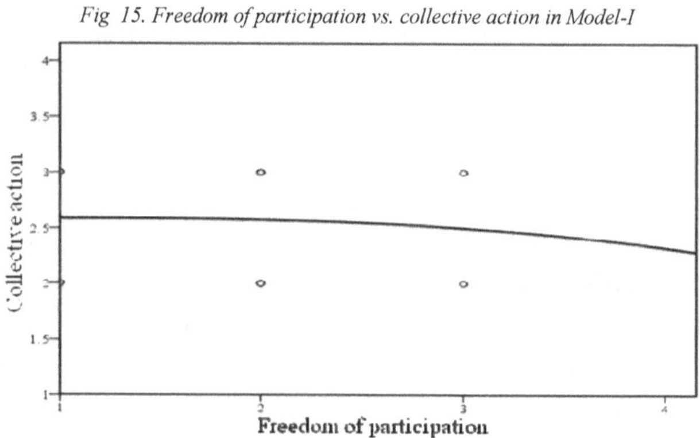

Fig 16. Freedom of participation vs. collective action in Model-II

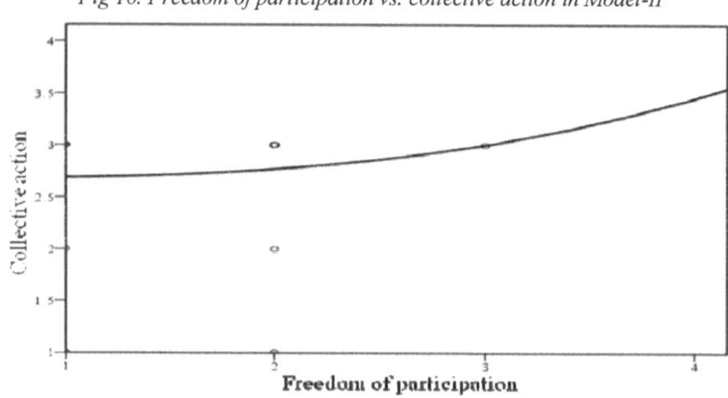

Fig 17. Freedom of participation vs. collective action in Model-III

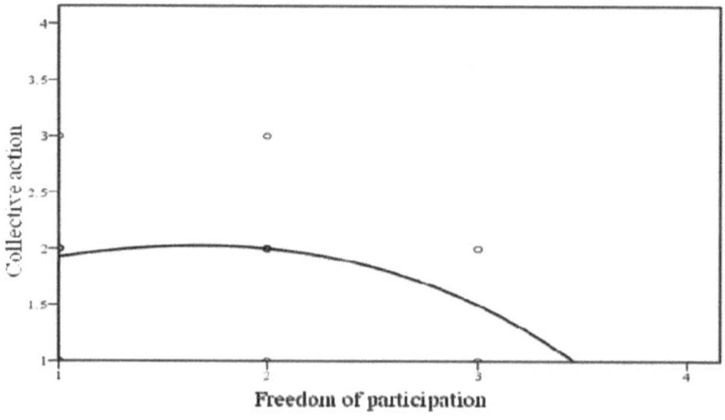

Source: Own compilation, 2009

4.6. Overall results

The present study analyses the different microcredit models in India with certain specific objectives. The study was conducted in the field with a set of framed hypotheses to test, and the results for the hypotheses are discussed below.

The first hypothesis framed states that the factors influencing the performance of SHGs differ from one model to the other. The variables, which are under the first, second, and third components of Model-I, are not necessarily under the first, second, and third components of other models, and vice versa. This emphasises that the direction and magnitude of variance of each variable in explaining the factor loadings of the components varies from one model to the other. It is clear from the findings of factor analysis that there are several factors influencing the performance. Further, the results of correlation analysis proved that there are several social and economic variables influencing the economic performance of the SHGs and that their level of influence is different from one model to the other. Supporting this, MNL regression analysis output showed that clear differences exist in the level of influence of variables on the economic performance of SHGs under three microcredit models. In addition, the outcome of categorical regression analysis enunciated that many factors are influencing the social performance of the SHGs at different levels under the three microcredit models. Hence, the hypothesis framed for the study is supported.

The other hypothesis put forth was that collective action differs with differences in the structural variables and is the driving mechanism for the difference in performance in different microcredit delivery models at the SHG level. The empirical findings from the curve-estimation technique for the selected structural variables like homogeneity of the group, age of the SHGs, and freedom of participation with collective action revealed that the level of collective action is different in the three microcredit SHG models, and it varies with the variation in the structural variables. Thus, the presented hypothesis is supported.

Another hypothesis formulated was that the performance of Self-Help Groups from Model-I is better than the performance of the Self-Help Groups of the other two microcredit delivery models. By considering the overall empirical evidence of the study and along with the experience perceived from respondents' interaction during the field survey by the researcher, the hypothesis is supported. It is deduced that with the confined variables and samples under study, the performance of the SHGs in

Model-I is better than the performance of SHGs of the other two microcredit delivery models in the study area. But the present study results contradict with the results of the study done in Kerala state (GOVERNMENT OF KERALA, 2004) and their findings indicate that the comparative performance of *Kudumbasree* is better than NGO-sponsored SHGs with respect to functioning and empowerment, indicating that the government-managed model is better than other models. The reason guessed at for the contradiction of results with the present study was difference in sample size, implementation procedures, and functional pattern of SHGs under the three models between Kerala and Karnataka state. Another reason might be because of changes in the structural, organisational, and promotional strategies, which can influence the performance of the group for the better.

While conducting the present research, several variable and specific hypotheses were framed to nail down the study objectives and were discussed earlier along with the analytical result. The test results are presented below.

4.7. Mapping of important variables for sustainable microcredit delivery model

Overall, from the present study on the performance of SHGs of different microcredit delivery models, we can clearly state that the performance of the groups depends on several of the social and economic factors of the group members and the group, along with other institutional factors like knowledge and support of the bank/government agency/NGO institutions of SHG linkage influence the performance of the SHGs under the three models. Based on the empirical findings of the study, important variables for achieving the sustainable performance of microcredit delivery models are lined up and classified under social, institutional, and economic factors and are depicted in Figure 18.

Table 17. List of formulated hypotheses tested in the study

Framed hypotheses	Tested results		
	Model-I	Model-II	Model-III
The higher the education of members is, the better the performance of SHGs	A	A	A
The higher the family income of members is, the better the performance of SHGs will be	A	A	A
The more the subsidy amount given, the better the performance of SHGs	A	R	A
The higher the total savings of members in SHGs, better is the performance of SHGs	A	A	A
The higher the savings amount collected per person per week is, better is the performance of SHGs	A	A	A
The more that loans are taken for IGA, the better is the performance of SHGs	A	R	R
The more that credit taken is higher than savings amount, the better the performance of SHGs	A	A	A
The longer the time duration available for repayment, the better the chances for repayment	A	A	A
The higher the satisfaction about the workings of the supporting institution is, the better the performance of SHGs	A	A	A
The more knowledge of SHG linkage to bank/NGO/ govt. agency acquired, the better the performance of SHGs	A	A	A
The higher the rate of attendance in meetings, the better is the performance of SHGs	A	A	A
The higher the level of members' participation, the better is the performance of SHGs	A	A	A
The higher the number of subgroups, the lower is the repayment	A	A	A
As the age of the SHG increases, the better the repayment is	A	A	A
The higher the transparency in SHG activities is, the better the performance	A	A	A
The lower the trust in other members in the group, the lower the performance	A	A	A
When fewer risks are involved in acquiring the credit, the better the performance	A	A	A
The lower the cost in acquiring the credit by SHGs is, the better the performance	R	R	R
The more there is homogeneity of group members, the better the collective action	R	A	A
As age of the SHGs increase, the better the collective action	A	R	A
The less freedom of participation exists, the lower the amount of collective action	A	A	R

Note: A- Accepted, R- Rejected. *Source: Own compilation, 2009*

Fig 18. Mapping of variables for sustainable performance of microcredit delivery models

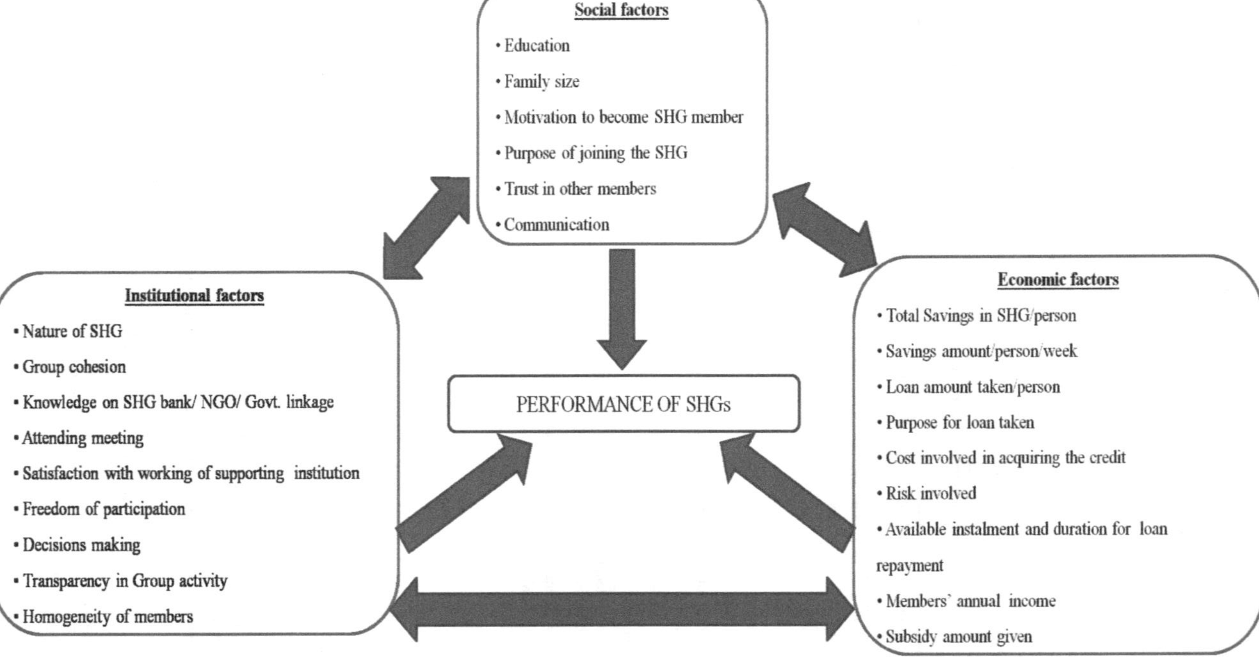

Source: Own compilation, 2009

Chapter 5 Summary and Conclusion

Being a largely populated country, India is one of the developing countries facing the serious challenges of poverty. One of the major causes of poverty in rural India is lack of access to productive assets and financial resources for both individuals and for communities. Microcredit has emerged and succeeded as a new paradigm for combating poverty and has become a major instrument for financial institutions to provide services for the rural poor. In Indian rural villages, neighbourhood groups are informally named with different local names, but widely called Self-Help Groups. These are informal groups of 10 to 20 members that have a common vision of the need and importance towards collective action (KHUN, 1985). Collective action among the rural communities has gained great momentum through SHGs. Since last decade, microcredit through SHGs has been used as a springboard to reach the rural poor to meet their financial demands in the present world (ROY, 1994 and OJHA, 2001). The peer group pressure is identified as a valuable collateral substitute, which has resulted in high levels of repayment. In the beginning, in India this approach has been extensively used only by the voluntary agencies (NGOs).

But presently, microcredit through SHGs is being practised in different ways and is grouped and monitored primarily under three models based on their linkage with the supporting institution – Model-I: bank-promoted; Model-II: government agency-promoted; Model-III: NGO-promoted. Each of these models is operating under a different framework of rules and regulations, starting with group formation. They also differ in the amount of government support, purpose of loan, amount of loan disbursement, interest rate, mode of repayment, purpose, functioning, etc., (UNESCO, 2004) and hence also differ in their performance and impact on its members. The microcredit through SHGs under these three models had a modest beginning and now has become "macro" in its approach and observed a wide variation in the shares of these implemented models. Hence, the present study attempts to examine the comparative performance and collective action of these three microcredit delivery models, with the main focus: (i) to study and compare the factors influencing the performance of different microcredit delivery models of Self-Help Groups by using multivariate techniques; (ii) to study the collective action and structural variables in different microcredit delivery models at Self-Help Group level.

The study was conducted in three *taluks* of the Davanagere district in Karnataka state (India). In the study area, three SHGs were randomly selected from each microcredit delivery model, thus a total of nine SHGs were studied. A further 10 members from each SHG were randomly selected, reaching a total of 90 members, and were interviewed with the help of a semi-structured questionnaire. The quantitative data collected is compiled and analysed using suitable statistical techniques to study the research objectives. The socio-economic profile of the respondents is studied using frequencies and percentages; it is observed that the members show no large differences in their profiles at the overall level between the three models. The outcomes of the study are summarised hereunder.

5.1. Summary

During the survey, data was collected from the sample members that were related to many variables, and the *Kruskal-Wallis* test is used to identify the variables, which differ significantly between the models. The results indicate that though the three models are working on the same population with the same objective, they differ significantly in many of the factors, which in turn can influence the performance of the SHGs under the three models. Furthermore, the variables are subjected to factor analysis by principle component extraction method, and all the models have three components explaining their extracted factor loadings. The extracted components in Model-I explain about 51.42 per cent of total variance extracted by the factor solutions, followed by Model-III (47.48%) and Model-II (45.81%). The results clearly indicate that each variable has its own loadings on respective components in all three models and that many of the variables differ from one to the other. The variables' loading on each component varies significantly both in sign and value from one model to the other. The variables under the first, second, and third component of Model-I are not necessarily under the first, second, and third component of the other models, and vice versa. This emphasises that direction and magnitude of variance of each variable in explaining the factor loadings of the components varies from one model to the other. This answers our first objective: comparing the factors influencing the performance of SHGs in three models.

In the study, based on review of literature and after gaining in-depth knowledge on the present research topic, loan repayment status of members and overall group functioning are used as dependent variables to measure the economic and social performance of the SHGs in three models. The relationships between the economic performance of the group and several predictors are studied using correlation analysis. The results reveal that several social and economic variables show different patterns of relationships with loan repayment status and, in turn, on economic performance of SHGs under the three models considered in the study.

Considering the statistical criteria, multivariate analysis is done to study the economic performance of SHGs under the three microcredit models, taking repayment status as dependent variable; since the dependent variable had multiple outcomes, it is fitted with multinomial logistic regression. The coefficients of explanatory variables are interpreted as the changes in the log-odds of the repayment status of the comparison group to the reference group associated with a unit change in the predictor variable, while other variables are held constant in the model. The fitted model with the limited statistical sample revealed that the model is significant at 10 per cent in Model-I with 28.365 chi-square value, whereas in Model-II and Model-III, the overall fit of MNL regression function is significant at 5 per cent with 57.561 and 57.330 chi-square values, respectively. The results revealed that in Model-I, the explanatory variables like amount of savings in SHG per person (X_4), loan amount taken per person (X_5), and satisfaction with the workings of the supporting institution (X_7) are the important factors influencing the repayment status of the members and are significant at the 5-per cent level; other predictors are not significant contributors to repayment status and, in turn, explain the performance of the SHG at the group level. In Model-II, except for the age of the SHG (X_3) and satisfaction with the workings of the supporting institution (X_7), all other predictors influence the repayment status and, in turn, the economic performance of the group significantly at the 5-per cent level and the age of the members at the 10-per cent level. In the case of Model-III, the predictor age of SHG (X_3) does not significantly influence repayment status. This is followed by satisfaction with the workings of the supporting institution (X_7), significant at the 10-per cent level, and the rest of the variables, significant at the 5-per cent level, in explaining the economic performance of the SHGs.

The social performance of an SHG was studied using categorical regression analysis with 12 selected independent variables and overall group functioning as a dependent variable, giving due consideration to the nature of variables. The standardised coefficients in the output explain the relationship between the predictor and the response variable. The output has given many meaningful insights like: (i) Groups formed based on neighbourhood will have better performance than groups formed based on other factors in Model-I and Model-III, and vice versa in Model-II; (ii) In all three models, the groups with the purpose for joining SHGs for financial security have increased social performance, followed by the SHGs formed for other purposes; (iii) The motivation factor for becoming an SHG member also influences the performance of the group –the highest performance is observed if motivated by neighbours, followed by, in order, motivated by friends, SHG members, officials of bank/government /NGO, relatives, or any other in Model-I, whereas it is vice versa in Model-II and Model-III; (iv) The groups with members always attending the meetings had better performance, followed by the groups where members attended meetings sometimes, rarely, and or never in Model-I, Model-II, and vice versa in Model-III, showing that equal responsibility of members in decision-making in the group and activeness of the group is higher in Model-I and Model-II when compared to Model-III.

Other additional outcomes of the social performance study were: (v) The social performance of the groups in all the models observed was highest where member participation was very active, followed by the performance of groups having actively, seldom, and never had freedom of participation, articulating the importance of freedom of participation of members for group performance; (vi) The performance of the group was found to be highest if the transparency in SHG activities was ensured always, followed by reduced performance if the transparency in SHG was sometime or never, inferring that transparency in functioning of the SHGs is an important factor in the performance of SHGs at the group level in all the models; (vii) Trust in members has a direct impact on social performance in all the models, performance of groups will be higher when the trust between members is very good and decreases as trust decreases; (viii) Better performance in all the models was observed more in the SHGs that took decisions based on the consensus, indicating that the cooperation and consent of all the members is equally important for the group performance; (ix) In all the models, it was observed that the less the risk involved in acquiring the credit, the higher the social performances of groups are and vice versa, indicating risk involved in acquiring the credit through an SHG is also a crucial factor; (x) The performance of SHGs was observed to be better in all three models when the cost involved in acquiring the credit was most expensive, compared to the lower cost in acquiring the credit from SHGs, inferring that the increased cost in getting credit helps the members understand the value of credit, thereby binding them more in the group to do better, in turn increasing the performance.

Later, the second objective – the collective action and structural variables in three microcredit delivery models – was studied. Collective action is complex and not easy to analyse to compare the behaviour of variables with it, hence in the midst of the available means, collective action is analysed with the selected variables, like homogeneity of members in the group, age of the SHGs, and freedom of participation, using a curve-estimation technique. The functional relationship between the variable and the collective action found that homogeneity of the group and freedom of participation fit a third-order function with collective action and a second-order function between age of the SHGs and collective action. Based on the study, the results articulated that collective action behaviour is multifaceted and the level of the collective action is different in all the three microcredit models with respect to the studied structural variables like members' backgrounds, stability in self-enforcement over time, and group functioning under free-rider situation. Thus underpinning, collective action behaviour depends mainly on the variation in the structural variable, and hence it differs in the SHGs of one microcredit model to the other.

From the overall study, it is observed that SHGs in Model-I perform better than SHGs of other models. It might be due to the differences in the supporting institutions and also it was ascertained as the self-enforcement of people in SHG formation, voluntary peer group binding, firm and deliberate liaison of members is more in Model-I SHG members than in other two microcredit models.

5.2. Conclusion

The analyses of quantitative data in the study lead to statistical conclusions that have shown significant differences between the models. Since the data is limited, it is difficult to generalise for a larger population. But it gives a partial picture of the three microcredit models in the study area. All three microcredit models have proved their ability in reaching the rural poor in a large and diverse country like India. Though they work in different modes and perform at different levels, they are indispensable in bringing the poor under a formal financial system.

However, it is clear from the study that there are several structural differences in the context, indicating the complexity in the models. Hence, it is suggested that these microcredit models should not be rigid and stagnant in their functioning, like other government departments. As time progresses, with the changing society the size, interests, and expectations of the targeted clients also change. Hence, while dealing with SHGs and microcredit, one has to know the difficulties and intricacies that exist in every specific context in which the SHG tries to achieve a better outcome. In each model, there are specific factors that predominantly influence the performance of the individual models, factors which – when adopted by other models – could enhance their performance. Hence, it is recommended that these microcredit models work interdependently in order to come up with better and new innovative approaches for future implementation. Thus, collective functioning of all three microcredit delivery models can improve the performance of SHGs.

The collective action in the group nurtures the performance of the models. Collective action behaviour is not generic, but context-specific, as it differs with the change in structural variables. Hence, due consideration to the collective action and structural variables by the supporting institutions is a prerequisite in all three models for the better execution of any SHG microcredit linkage.

5.3. Implications of the study

1. It is clear from the study that banks are the key lending agencies in all three microcredit models. As the microcredit programme has become "macro" in its approach, it is recommended that the banks bring in the appropriate organisational changes, with a special focus on group lending and microcredit, so that they can play a proactive role at the grassroots level to enhance the performance of SHGs, irrespective of the three models.
2. During the study, it was observed that performance was better in the SHGs comprising members who are satisfied with the workings of their supporting institutions. Hence, it is suggested to widely streamline the support of the mainstream institutions like banks, NGOs, and government agencies that are

involved in the microcredit models for strategic capacity-building of SHG members.

3. It is observed during the study that bank-promoted SHGs in Model-I have formed much larger federation, which has eased capacity-building, income-generation activity (IGA) training, dissemination of information, and also reaching the groups. Hence, it is recommended that NGOs and government agencies form similar federations of SHGs in the other two models to better achieve their goals.
4. The results of the study reveal that cohesion, cooperation, and consent of all the members, and knowledge of the SHG linkages, are relatively more influential than other factors on group performance. Thus, it is recommended for all the microcredit delivery models to make members aware of their group activities and give regular updates on the SHG microcredit programme.
5. It is clear from the results of collective action analysed in the study that NGOs in Model-III succeeded in monitoring the normal group functioning and in creating better understanding between the group members as and when required. But in Model-II, this feature is lacking on the part of government agencies. Hence, it is advised for government agencies to adopt similar patterns of monitoring SHGs.
6. Based on the results of the present study, important variables are identified, consolidated, and mapped as social factors, economic factors, and institutional factors that are required for a sustainable microcredit model. Hitherto, it is recommended to emphasise these mapped variables for the development of sustainable microcredit models.
7. It was observed during the study that several SHGs have successfully completed few cycles of borrowing and repayment of credit. These group members have realised the importance of credit for productive purposes. They realised that facilitating microcredit alone will not reduce poverty. In addition, support from these institutions in the form of forward and backward market linkage for their products produced from IGA is expected. Hence, it is recommended for banks, government agencies, and NGOs to guide and help the members with diversified means to start IGAs to enable them to escape their vulnerability.

5.4. Further research scope

1. The present study examined and compared the factors influencing the performance of different microcredit delivery models at the SHG level. Similarly, a full-scale study including SHGs and the supporting institutions in the three microcredit models can be conducted to scale up the sustainable microcredit delivery models realistically at the "macro" and "micro" levels to reach the poor.
2. The present study was confined to only one district with a limited sample size and limited number of variables due to constraints of the student research. Hence, similar studies with different dimensions of objectives considering more variables can be undertaken on a wider scale to come up with more generic and comprehensive conclusions.
3. A similar study can also be conducted on urban microcredit models, which are facing emerging challenges in combating urban poverty.

5.5. Limitations of the study

It was a single student investigation that placed limitations on time and other resources at the student's disposal. This led to the purposive selection of the locale of the study. The study is based on the expressed opinions of the respondents, which may be biased. In spite of the researcher's efforts to make them as objective as possible, the possibility of some errors creeping in can not be ruled out.

The study was confined to only three *taluks* of the Davanagere district in Karnataka (India) with few selected variables. Thus, a generalisation made based on the findings of the present study may have only limited application in the non-study area as differences exist from region to region. An extensive study covering a larger area with more variables for comprehensive and more generic findings could have been possible in an unconstrained situation. Study on the bylaws of the SHGs and supporting institutions, and also the analysis of the institutional framework of these models, would have further strengthened the findings of the present study.

References

ADOLPH B., 2003, The role of Self help Groups in rural non-farm employment, rural non-farm economy: Access factors. *Discussion paper*, Department of International Development, Natural Resource Institute.

AGARWAL, A., 2000, Small is beautiful, but is larger better? Forest management institutions in the Kumoan Himalaya, India. Pp. 57–86 in *People and forests: communities, institutions and governance*, eds. C. Gidson, M. McKean, and E. Ostrom. Cambridge, Mass.: MIT Press.

AGARWAL, A., 2001, Common property institutions and sustainable governance of resources. *World Development* 29(10): 1623–1648.

AGARWAL, A., 2002, "Common resources and institutional sustainability." Pp. 41-85 in *The drama of the commons. National Research Council, Committee on the Human Dimensions of Global Change*, eds. E. Ostrom, T. Dietz, N. Dolšak, P.C. Stern, S. Stonich, and E. Weber. Washington, DC: National Academy Press.

AGRESTI, A., 1996, An introduction to categorical data analysis. New York: John Wiley.

AICRP, 2001, *Database on rural women and indigenous knowledge*. Report on extension component 1996-2001. Indian Council of Agricultural Research, New Delhi.

ALDRICH, J.H., and NELSON F.E., 1984, Sage University Paper Series on Quantitative applications in the social sciences. Beverly Hills, California.

ANITA KUMARI, 2002, Role of rural women in decision making in house hold activities in Bihar. *Maharashtra Journal of Extension Education* XX (1).

ARDENER, S., 1964, The comparative study of rotating credit associations. *Journal of Royal Anthropological Institute* XCIV(2): 201–229.

ATHENA, C., 2009, A study on the levels of living of Self Help Groups in Coimbatore district, Tamil-nadu. Language in India, Strength for today and bright hope for tomorrow. Vol. 9: 1, Feb. ISSN 1930-2940.

BALASUBRAMANIAN, R., and SELVARAJ, K.N., 2003, Poverty, private property and common pool resource management. The case of irrigation tanks in South Asia. SANDEE working paper, No. 2-03. Kathmandu, Nepal.

BARDHAN, D., and DABAS Y.P.S., 2007, Microfinance initiatives through Self Help Groups: Some issues. *Agricultural Extension Review* (January-June).

BHARATHI, R.A., 2005, Assessment of Self Help Groups promoted under NATP on empowerment of women in agriculture. M.Sc. Thesis, Department of Extension and Communication Management, University of Agricultural Sciences, Dharwad.

BRIGHT H., 2006, Access for all-building inclusive financial systems, CGAP, capturing 10 years of CGAP experience-financial service providers: The micro level, IDBI.

CAMERER, C.F., 2003, *Behavioural game theory: Experiments in strategic interaction.* Princeton, NJ: Princeton University Press.

CETRON, M.J., 2004, World future 2004 – Creating the future now, prospects for China and India in the 21st century. Forecast International.

CGAP, 2005, CGAP report – Consultative group to assist the poorest.

CGAP, 2007, Sustainability of Self Help Groups in India: Two analyses. Occasional paper, CGAP. Data from NABARD: No. 12.

CHAWLA, O.P., and PATEL, K.V., 1987, Change and development in the village-role of self help organisations. *Prajnan* 16(3): 283–298.

COLE, N. S., 1987, *Task role communication and ecology of mind.* San Francisco; Chandler Publication C.

DANIEL, C., AND WOOD, F.S., 1999, *Fitting equations to data: Computer analysis of multifactor data.* 2nd edition. NY: Wiley-Interscience. A leading text on curve estimation, going beyond the capabilities of the SPSS Curve Estimation module.

DIETZ, T., OSTROM, E., and STERN, P., 2003, The struggle to govern the commons. *Science* 302: 1907–12.

DWARAKINATH, B. R., 1997, Towards creating a participatory self-help credit co-operative. *National seminar on rediscovering co-operation.* Nov. 19–21, IRMA, 2: 216–236.

ELLERMAN D., 2008, "Social funds and microfinance programmes. Paper presented by David Ellerman. The World Bank at Fundamental Conundrum of Overseas Development at the Institute of Development Policy & Movement. University of Antwerp, Belgium, March 4.

FADIGA, M.L., and FADIGA STEWART, L. A., 2004, Collective action and informal financial institutions: An empirical analysis of rotating and savings credit associations (ROSCAs) in Senegal. Paper presented at the *American of Agricultural Economics Association*, annual meeting. Denver, Colorado, August 1–4.

FEDERAL RESEARCH DIVISION REPORT, 2004, Library of Congress – Federal Research Division. Country Profile: India, December.

FUDENBERG, D., and MASKIN, E., 1986, The folk theorem in repeated games with discounting or with incomplete information. *Econometrica* 54(3): 533–54.

GABA, G., and ABHA, A., 2003, Perception of women about their status as members of selected Self help Groups of Udham singh nagar district. Pantnagar, *Journal of research* vol. 1 (June).

GIBSON, C., WILLIAMS, J., and OSTROM, E., 2005, "Local enforcement and better forests." *World Development* 33(2): 273–284.

GLOBAL MONITORING REPORT, 2004, Global Monitoring Report, Millennium Development Goals, policies and actions for achieving the Millennium Development Goals and related outcomes.

GOVERNMENT OF INDIA, 2007, *Government of India Report.*

GOVERNMENT OF JHARKHAND, 2007, Study on Self Help Groups – Microcredit: An innovative way to help poor people improve their lives.

GOVERNMENT OF KARNATAKA, 1993, Population Centre, Socio-Economic and Demographic Profile of Karnataka, Bangalore.

GOVERNMENT OF KARNATAKA, 2004, *Government of Karnataka Report.*

GOVERNMENT OF KARNATAKA, 2008, Davanagere district at a glance, Office of District Statistical Officer, ZP, Davanagere.

GOVERNMENT OF KERALA, 2004, A comparative study of Self Help Groups organized and promoted by NGOs and *Kudumbasree* (A government-organised NGO) in Kerala. Government of Kerala.

HAGENBUCH, W., 1958, *Social economics.* Nishet and Company, Cambridge, Britain.

HAIR J.F., ANDERSON, R.E., TATHAM, R.L., and WILLIAM, C.B., 2005, Multivariate data analysis, fifth addition, Pearson Education Pte., Ltd.

HANSTAD, T., BROWN, J., and PROSTERMAN, R., 2002, Larger homestead plots as land reform – International experiences and analysis from Karnataka. *Economic and Political Weekly.*

HARDIN, R., 1976, "Group provision of step goods." *Behavioural Science* 21: 101–106.

HARDIN, R., 1982, *Collective* action. Baltimore, MD: Johns Hopkins University Press.

HARE, T., 1976, *Leadership style and people.* Washington, USA: McGraw Hill.

HARMAN, H.H., 1968, *Modern factor analysis*. Chicago: The University of Chicago Press.

HARPER, M., 1996, Self Help Groups – Some issues from India. *Small Enterprise Development* 7(2).

HAYES, T.M., and OSTROM, E., 2005, "Conserving the world's forests: Are protected areas the only way?" *Indiana Law Review* 37(3): 595–617.

HEATHER, M., and WEISS, J., 2006, Modalities of microfinance delivery in Asia and Latin America: Lessons for China. *China and World Economy* 14(1): 30–43.

HEMALATHA PRASAD, C., and OM PRAKASH, 1997, Sustainable employment for women – Mahila Chetna Manch shows the way. *Gramin vikas Newsletter* 13(6): 13–15.

HOSAMANI, 1993, Study on knowledge of general health practices of rural women and their communication behaviour. Bailhongal, Karnataka. M.Sc. (Agri.) Thesis, University of Agricultural Sciences, Dharwad.

IFAD, 2007, Microfinance: Macro benefits. Rome: International Fund for Agriculture (IFAD).

INDIAN BANK, 1996, Financing Self Help Groups "Swayam Seva". Madras: Indian Bank Central Office.

JAIN, R., and KUHAWALA, R.K., 2004, Self Help Groups' issues and constraints. *Indian Journal of Extension Education* Vol. XXXX(3&4): 58–60.

JAYARAMAN, B., 2001, Micro-finance retrospect and prospects. Occasional paper – Microfinance programmes other country experiences, NABARD.

JONES, E. C., 2004, Wealth-based trust and the development of collective action. *World Development* 32(4): 691-711.

JUSTUS, E. R., and MOHIBA, M., 2000, Participatory micro enterprises: A case study of PASA. *Kurukshetra: Journal of Rural Development* 49(3):40–4.

KABIR, H., 2002, The experience revolution and the Grameen Bank experience in Bangladesh. *Financial Markets Institutions and Instruments* 11(3).

KARMAKAR, K.G., 1998, SHGs in Orissa – Some conceptual issues. *Prajnan* 26 (2): 123–131.

KARUNA, K.K.M., MANJUNATH, L., GEETHA, S.C., and ASHALATHA, 2006, A study on performance of women Self Help Groups of north Karnataka. University of Agricultural Sciences, Dharwad.

KERR, N.L., and KAUFMAN-GILLILAND, C.M., 1994, Communication, commitment and co-operation in social dilemmas. *Journal of Personality and Social Psychology* 66: 513–29.

KHUN, J., 1985, The role of non-governmental organisations is promoting Self Help Organisation. Seminar papers, Druchari Tranz, Paffernholz Bomheins, p. 265.

KUMARAN, K.P., 1997, Self Help Groups: An alternative to institutional credit to the poor: A case study of Andhra Pradesh. *Journal of Rural Development* 16(3): 515–530.

LEDGERWOOD, J., 1999, "Sustainable banking with the poor; an institutional and financial perspective," Microfinance Handbook. Washington, DC: The World Bank.

LICHBACH, M.I., 1996, *The Cooperator's Dilemma.* Ann Arbor: University of Michigan Press.

LONG, S.J., 1997, Regression models for categorical and limited dependent variables. Thousand Oaks, CA: Sage Publications.

LOUIS, H.G.S., CORNELIS, G.V.K., and PAVEL, S., 2002, Institutions of sustainability in central and eastern European countries. Paper presented at Xth EAAE congress *Exploring diversity in the European agri-food system*, Zaragoza, Spain, 28–31 August.

MAHAPATRA, B.C., DAS, B.K., and MOHANTHI, B.P., 1997, Agricultural and social development in Jagannathapur village of Orissa – A case study. *Journal of Rural Development* 16(3): 531–539.

MAHAPATRA, K., and KANT, S., 2005, Tropical deforestation: A multinomial logistic model and some country-specific policy prescriptions. *Forest Policy and Economics* 7: 1–24.

MANGASRI, K., 1999, Empowerment of DWCRA groups in Ranga Reddy district of Andhra Pradesh. Ph.D. Thesis, ANGARAU, Hyderabad, Andhra Pradesh.

MANOHAR, K.M., SHOBHA, V., and RAO, B.J., 1981, Women construction workers of Warangal. *Economic and Political Weekly* 16(4): 97–99.

MARWELL, G., and OLIVER, P.E., 1993, *The critical mass in collective action: A micro-social theory*. New York: Cambridge University Press.

MEENA, S., and INTODIA, S.L., 1994, Women empowerment for sustainable agriculture development – Empowerment and gender gap reduction among women farmers of north India. Government of India.

MENARD, S., 2002, Applied logistic regression analysis, 2nd edition. Thousand Oaks, CA: Sage Publications series: Quantitative applications in the social sciences, no. 106. First ed. 1995.

MURUGAN, K.R., and DHARMALINGAM, B., 2000, Self Help Groups – New women's movement in Tamil nadu. *Social Welfare* 47: 9–12.

NABARD, 1995, Linking SHGs with banks – An Indian experience. NABARD Bombay, pp. 1–25.

NABARD, 2007, Annual Report for 2006-2007. District NABARD Branches, Dharwad, Karnataka.

NABARD, 2009, Potential linked Credit plan 2009-10, National Bank for agriculture and rural development, Davanagere district, Karnataka regional office, Bangalore.

NAILA, K., 2005, Is microfinance a "magic bullet" for women's empowerment? Analysis of findings from South Asia. *Economic and political weekly*, 4709–4718.

NARAYANASWAMY, B., NARAYANA GOWDA, K., and NAGARAJA, G.N., 2007, Performance of Self Help Groups of Karnataka in farm activities. Bio-resource complex (NBDB). College of agriculture, Bangalore. *Karnataka Journal of Agricultural Sciences* 20(1): 85–88.

NCEUS, 2007, National Commission for Enterprises in the unorganized sector report, http://www.reuters.com.

NEILS, H., and ROBERT L., 2007, The empirics of microfinance: What do we know? *The Economic Journal* 117(Feb): F1–F10.

NIXTON II, 1979, *The small group*. New Jersey: Prentice Hall Inc., Englewool diffs. 4: 108–156.

NORUSIS, M., 2004, *SPSS 13.0 advanced statistical procedures companion*. Upper Saddle-River, N.J.: Prentice Hall, Inc.

NORUSIS, M.J., 1999, SPSS regression models 10.0. Chicago, Illinois: SPSS Inc.

NSSO, 2006, NSSO data – National sample survey organisation. Ministry of Statistics and Programme Implementation, Government of India.

OJHA, R.K., 2001, Self Help Groups and rural employment. *Yojana: A Development Monthly* 45(2): 20–3.

OSLON, M., 1965, The logic of collective action. Public goods and the theory of groups. Cambridge, Mass: Cambridge University Press.

OSTROM, E., 2001, "Social dilemmas and human behavior." In *Economics in nature: Social dilemmas, mate choice and biological markets*, edited by R. Noë, J. Van Hooff, and P. Hammerstein. Cambridge: Cambridge University Press, pp. 21–41.

OSTROM, E., 2007, Collective action and local development processes. In *Sociologica* 3/2007, doi: 10.2383/25950. Available online at: http://www.sociologica.mulino.it/journal/articlefulltext/index/Article/Journal:ARTICLE:113#.

OSTROM, E.R., GARDNER, and WALKER, J., 1994, *Rules, games and common-pool resources*. Ann Arbor: University of Michigan Press.

PANDA, A.K., and MISHRA, A.K., 1996, SHG – Informal co-operatives in Orissa. Rediscovering co-operation. IRMA, Anand, Gujarat, 2: 216–235.

PLANNING COMMISSION, 2007, Planning Commission, poverty estimates. Government of India.

POTEETE, R. A., and OSTROM, E., 2003, In pursuit of comparable concepts and data about collective action. CAPRI working paper, No. 29, CGIAR system-wide programme on collective action and property rights. IFPRI research programme workshop on political theory and policy analysis. Indiana University.

POTEETE, R. A., and OSTROM, E., 2004, Heterogeneity, group size and collective action: The role of institutions in forest management. *Review, Fernand Braudel Center*. Vol. XXVII.

PRASAD, C.H., 1998, Implementation process of women development programme (IFAD) – An experimental model. *Journal of Rural Development* 17(4): 779–791.

PRATT, J. W., 1987, Dividing the indivisible: Using simple symmetry to partition variance explained. *Proceedings of the Second International Conference in Statistics*, eds. T. Pukkila, and S. Puntanen. Tampere, Finland: University of Tampere.

PUHAZHENDI, V., and JAYARAMAN, B., 1999, Increasing women's participation and employment generation among the poor – An approach through informal groups. *National Bank News Review* 15(4): 55–62.

PURNIMA, K.S., and NARAYANA REDDY, G.V., 2007, Indicators of effectiveness of women Self Help Groups in Andhra Pradesh. Research Note. *Journal of Research* ANGRAU 35(2): 93–96.

QAZI, M., 1999, Self Help Groups – A novel approach to rural development. *State Bank of India Monthly Review* 36(9): 460–465.

RAJAGOPALAN, B.K., 1998, SHGs and social defence. *Social welfare,* pp. 30–34.

RAKESH, MALHOTRA, 2005, NABARD – District development manager, NABARD, Bareilly, India.

RANGI, P.S., SINDHU, M.S., and HARJIT, SINGH, 2002, Economic empowerment of rural women through Self Help Groups: A case study of Fategarh Sahib district (Punjab). *Man and development* 24(3): 65–78.

RAO, K., 1994, Self Help Group and credit. *Artha vijnana* 36(3): 194–208.

RBI, 2007, Revisiting bank linked Self Help Groups – A study of Rajasthan state, RBI occasional paper, Monsoon 2007, by Navin Bhatia, DGM, RBI, Mumbai.

REDDY, C.S., 2007, Self Help Group – Bank linkage programme. A recurrent study in Andhra Pradesh. APMAS, Hyderabad.

RENUKARYA, C.K., 2004, Integrated quantitative analysis to assess the performance of SHGs in India. ISTR Sixth International Conference, *Contesting citizenship and civil society in a divided world,* Toronto, Canada.

ROBERT, C., 2005, "Microfinance and sustainability: International experiences and lessons for India." Conference paper for NABARD workshop, *Microfinance: Challenges for the Future.* New Delhi, 3–6 May.

ROUL, S., 1996a, Co-operative in the emerging contest. National seminar on rediscovering co-operation, IRMA, Anand.

ROUL, S., 1996b, Self Help Groups as an alternative model. National seminar on rediscovering co-operation, 19–21 Nov., IRMA, 2: 249–261.

ROY, D.K., 1994, Peasant movements grass root mobilization and empowerment of rural women: Some sociological observation. *Women's Link* 4(4): 17–8.

ROYAL TROPICAL INSTITUTE, 1987, Royal Tropical Institute – Rural economic development and food security, Amsterdam, Netherlands.

SA-DHAN, 2007, Maturing microfinance – Emerging challenges. Sa-Dhan. The Association of Community Development finance institutions.

SA-DHAN, 2008, The Bharat microfinance report, *Quick Data 2008*. Sa-Dhan. The Association of Community Development finance institutions.

SANKANAGOUDAR, S.K., 1991, Value orientation and socio-economic characteristics of women of Dharwad district. M.Sc. (Agri.) Thesis, University of Agricultural Sciences, Dharwad.

SARADA, O., SHIVAMURTHY, M., and SURESHA, S.V., 2008, Facilitating structural and functional characteristics on the level of empowerment of rural women Self Help Groups. *Mysore Journal of Agricultural Sciences* 42(2): 323–326.

SIMANOWITZ, A., NKUNA, B., and KASIM, S., 1999, Overcoming the obstacles of identifying the poorest families: Using Participatory Wealth Ranking (PWR), the Cashpor House Index (CHI), and other measurements to identify and encourage the participation of the poorest families. Meeting of councils plenary papers.

SINGH, S., 1995, Self Help Groups in Indian Agribusiness – Replications from case studies. *Artha vijnana* 37(4): 380–388.

SINGH, Y.K., KAUSHAL, S.K., and GAUTHAM, S.S., 2007, Performance of women's Self Help Groups (SHGs) in Moradabad district, Uttara Pradesh. *International Journal of Rural Studies (IJRS)* 14(2), ISSN 1023-2001.

SMITH, C., and FREEDMAN, A., 1972, *Voluntary associations: Perspective on the literature.* Cambridge, Mass: Harvard University Press.

SNOW D. R., and BUSS T. F., 2001, Development and the role of microcredit. *Policy Studies Journal* 29(2): 296–307.

SRINIVASAN N., 2008, *Microfinance India*, State of the sector report 2008. SAGE Publications.

SRIVASTAVA, R. S., 2002, Anti-poverty programmes in Uttar Pradesh: An evaluation. Commissioned by the Planning Commission, Government of India.

STAR, 2008, Star Report. The Daily, Dhaka: Transcraft Limited.

STATE FOR INTERNATIONAL DEVELOPMENT REPORT, 2000, Eliminating World Poverty: Making globalisation work for the poor. White paper on international development. Presented to Parliament by the Secretary of State for International Development by Command of Her Majesty, December.

SUDHARANI, K., 2002, SHGs, microcredit and empowerment. *Social Welfare* 49(11): 22–23.

TANKHA, A., 2002, Self Help Group as financial intermediaries in India: Cost of promotion, sustainability and impact. Sa-Dhan, New Delhi. A study report prepared for ICCO and Cordaid, The Netherlands, August.

UNESCO, 2004, Annual Report – UNESCO, United Nations Educational Scientific and Cultural Organization.

UNFPA, 2006, From Microfinance to macro change. Integrating health, education and microfinance to empower women and reduce poverty. Microcredit Summit Campaign, New York.

USHARANI, R., 1999, A study on adoption of women beneficiaries towards DWRCA and benefits derived in Vizianagaram district, Andhra Pradesh. M.Sc. Thesis, University of Agricultural Sciences, Dharwad.

VAN BASTELAER, T., 2000, Does social capital Facilitate the poor's access to credit? A review of the microeconomic literature. Social Capital Initiative, Working Paper No. 8.

VERHAGEN, K., 1987, Self Help Promotion – Challenge to the NGO community. Royal Tropical Institute, Amsterdam, Netherlands.

WORLD BANK, 1995, *World Development Report 1994-95*. Washington DC: World Bank.

WORLD BANK, 2000, World Development Report 2000-01: Attacking Poverty. Washington DC: World Bank.

WORLD BANK, 2008, World Development Report 2007-08: Agriculture for development. Washington DC: World Bank.

Photos showing SHG members of the study area

Photo 1. SHG member involved in IGA and the raw materials used and products prepared for market.

Photo 2. Members of SHG who are involved in Group IGA.

Photo 3. SHG members' participation in capacity-building programme.

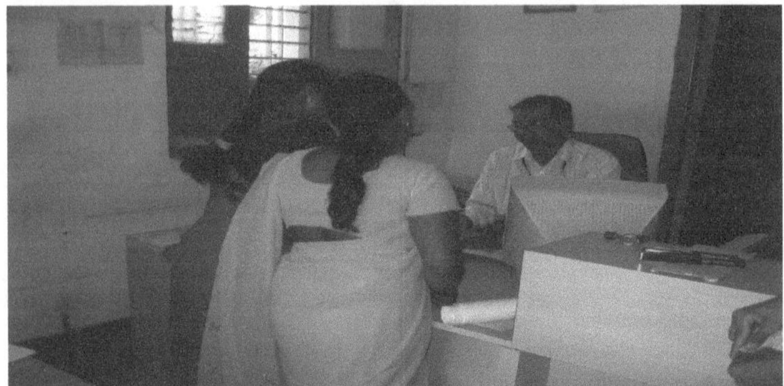

Photo 4. SHG members interacting with bank officials.

Photo 5. SHG members with their bank books.

Photo 6. Researcher interaction with the SHG members.

Photo 7. SHG group leader giving group information.

Photo 8. 5th generation hoping for empowerment through SHG and microcredit.

Annexures

Annexure 1. NGO profile in Davanagere district

Name of the NGO	Area of operation	No. of SHGs promoted	SHGs credit linked
Baduku swayam seva samsthe	Jagalur	200	185
Guri samsthe	Davanagere	45	NA
Socio-Economic Education Development Society (SEEDS)	Harapanahalli	200	130
Prayog Spandana	Honnali	100	60
REACH,	Harapanahalli	150	100
Vimukthi VIdhya Samsthe	Channagiri	100	70
Ekalavya Project	Davanagere	115	80
Pragathi Society for Rural Development	Channagiri	100	50
Renukadevi Women and Child Development Foundation	Davanagere	320	220
Action Aid Karnataka Project	Jagalur	-	-
Spoorthy	Channagiri	350	250
Maitri Association	Honnali	50	30
Gnanjyothi vidhya saumsthe	Davanagere Tq	350	250
Prazwala	Channagiri	70	-
Asare RUDSET	Honnali	80	50
Sankalpa	Davanagere Tq	65	35
ICDO	Davanagere	250	100

Annexure 2. Number of households in study area

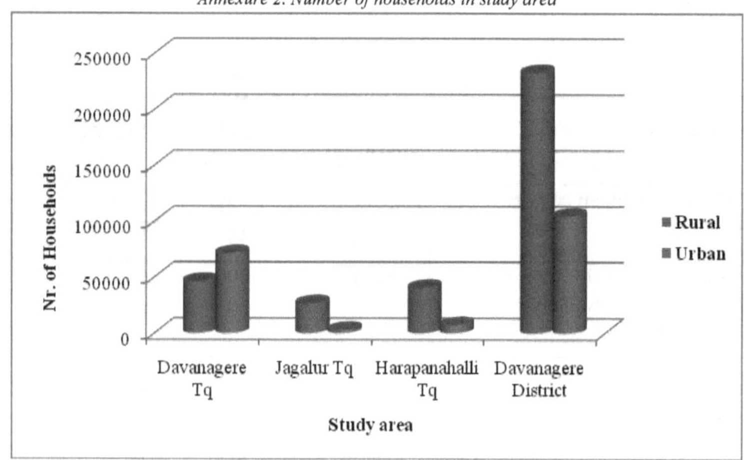

Annexure 3. Rural-urban population in the study area

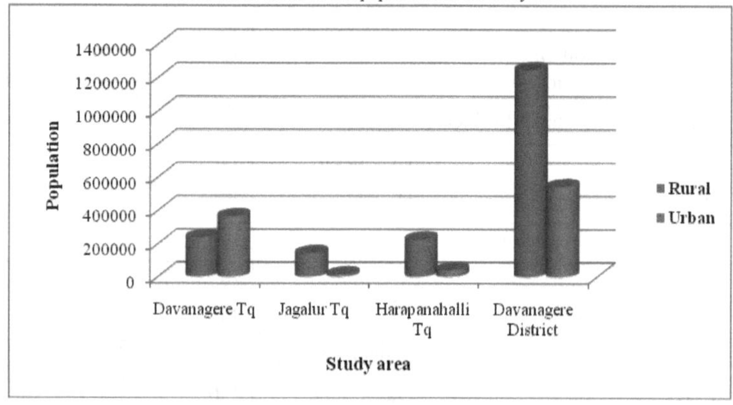

Annexure 4. Literacy rate (%) in the study area

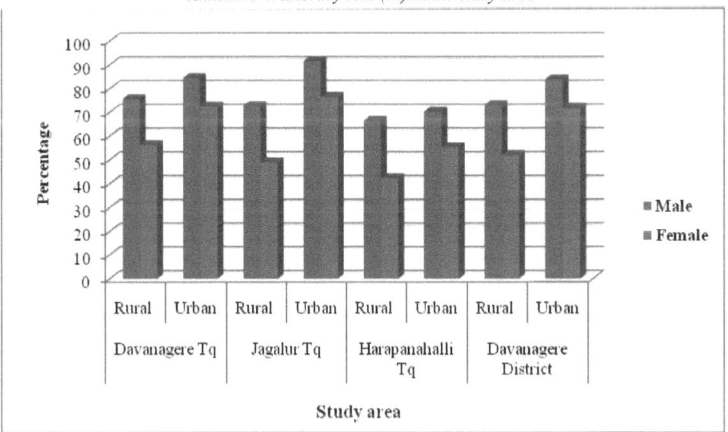

Annexure 5. Working population profile of the study area

Annexure 6. Flow chart showing sampling framework

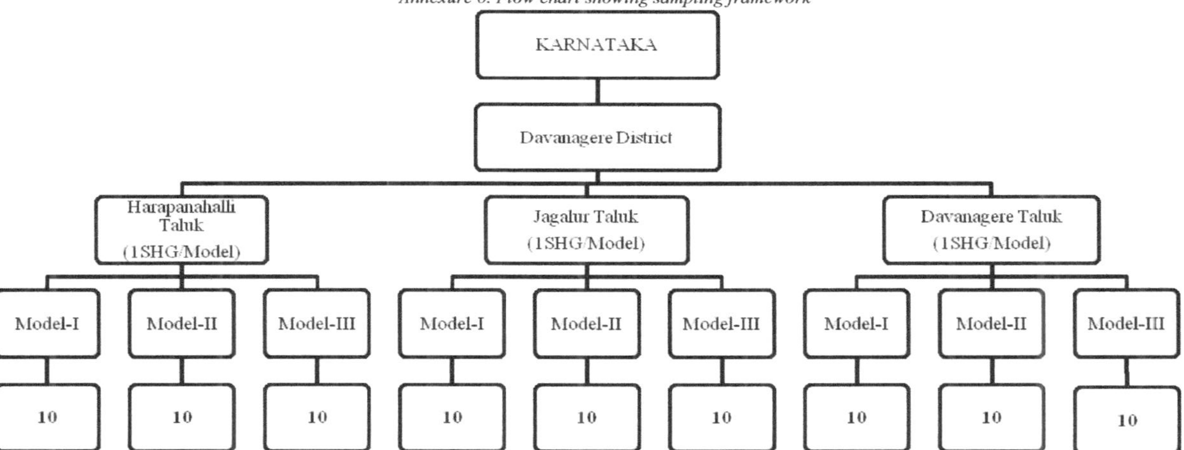

Annexure 7. MNL regression results showing Exp (β) values for the explanatory variables

Independent variables	Dependent: Repayment status		
	Exp(β)		
	Model-I	Model-II	Model-III
Full paid vs. not started			
Intercept			
X_1	1.011	1.279	0.927
X_2	0.857	0.087	0.239
X_3	2.44	1.063E+13	1.034E+11
X_4	1009781694	0.950	0.065
X_5	1.008	0.988	0.997
X_6	1.106	0.015	50325.35
X_7	2.557	31.423	1.092
Regularly paid vs. not started			
Intercept			
X_1	1.013	1.147	0.83
X_2	0.035	0.583	0.645
X_3	1037.928	55456.531	7413.07
X_4	495.869	0.983	0.255
X_5	1.010	0.999	1.001
X_6	7.312E-07	0.00002684	31220000000
X_7	8.743	4.842	0.307
Irregularly paid vs. not started			
Intercept			
X_1	0.942	0.016	0.231
X_2	0.981	1341.318	15.172
X_3	18100000	3.467E+42	1.29E+37
X_4	3.519E-09	0.776	5.807
X_5	1.007	0.973	1.002
X_6	2.331E-07	5.104E-08	1.208E+13
X_7	0.431	256300000	0.023

Source: Own compilation, 2009

Annexure 8. The R^2 value and test statistic of curve estimation for structural variables vs. collective action of groups

Structural variables/ Collective action	Model-I		Model-II		Model-III	
	R^2	Sig.	R^2	Sig.	R^2	Sig.
Members' backgrounds	0.152	0.109	0.141	0.041	0.127	0.053
Age of the SHG	0.318	0.006	0.140	0.120	0.111	0.072
Freedom of participation	0.261	0.0930	0.164	0.081	0.237	0.164

Source: Own compilation, 2009

Annexure 9. Questionnaire for SHG Member

The Performance of Microcredit Organisations – A Comparative Perspective

Schedule number:___________ Date:

1. Name of the SHG:
2. Village:
3. **SHG is sponsored by: Bank-1, Government-2, NGO-3**
4. **Socio-economic information:**

4.1 Name of the respondent:________________

4.2 Age:________

4.3 Sex: Male-1, Female-2

4.4 Religion:
Hindu-1, Muslim-2, Christian-3, Other-4

4.5 Caste:
General-1, SC/St-2, OBC-3, Other-4

4.6 Marital Status:
Single-1, Married-2, Widow/er-3, Divorcee -4

4.7 Education:
Illiterate-1, Primary only-2, Up to SSLC-3, PUC-4, Degree holder-5, Diploma-6, P.G. Degree-7

4.8 Main Occupation:
Agriculture-1, Agri-labour-2, Non-agri-labourers-3, Small business-4,

Housewife-5, Govt. service-6, Private service-7, Craftsman-8, Other-9

Any subsidiary occupation:____________________

4.9 Type of family:
Nuclear-1, Joint-2

Male adults: _______, Female adults:________,

Male children:______, Female children:______

4.10 Average monthly income of the family (approximately): INR
Less than 500-**1**, 500 to 1,000-**2**, 1,001 to 2,000-**3**, 2,001 to 3,000-**4**,

3,001 to 4,000-**5**, 4,001 to 5,000-**6**, more than 5,000-**7**.

4.11 Ownership of house:
Own-1, Rented-2

5. SHGs membership information:

5.1 When did you join SHG?

Month: _____, Year: _______

5.2 How old is your SHG? __________

5.3 Who motivated you to become the member of SHG?

Neighbours-1, Friends-2, SHG members-3, Officials of: NGO-4/bank-5/government-6
Relatives-7, Any other (specify)-8 __________ __________

5.4 Do all who approach SHG get SHG membership?
Yes-1, No-2
If no, list the selection criteria:
1.
2.
3.

5.5 Who will make decision on selecting or giving SHG membership?
All existing members-1, Office bearers-2,
Other-3: (specify)________

5.6 Nature of SHG:
Caste-based-1, Occupation-based-2, Age-based-3, Location-based-4

5.7 Your designation in your SHG:
Member-1, Office bearer-2

5.8 Purpose for joining the SHG:
Financial security-1, Enhancing social status-2, Increase social participation-3,
To increase family business-4, Other-5 (specify):____________

6. SHGs working dynamics:

6.1 Attending the meetings:
Always-1, Sometimes-2, Rarely-3, Never-4

6.2 Frequency of meetings held:
Weekly-1, Bi-weekly-2, Monthly-3, Bi-monthly-4, More than that (specify)

6.3 Do all the members attend the meetings regularly?
Yes-1, No-2

If no, reason:________________

6.4 Is attending meetings required?
Voluntary-1, Compulsory -2

6.5 How many members are there in SHG?____________
6.6 Any dropouts in your SHG?
Yes-1, No-2

If yes, number:__________,

Reasons for dropping out:____________, ___________

6.7 Is there any action taken against the member who is not involved in any of the SHG activities?
Yes-1, No-2
If yes, list the action taken:____________________________
If no, list the reasons:_______________________

Are the records like attendance registers, account books, reports maintained properly?
Yes-1, No-2, Do not know-3
If yes,
Who maintains them?__________

6.8 Have you examined any of these during last six months?
Yes-1, No-2
6.9 If yes, how are they?
Marginal-1, Below average-2, Average-3, Above average-4, Complete and up to date-5, Virtually no errors-6

6.10 What is the savings amount collected from one member?
Amount Rs.:________; Is it a fixed amount? Yes-1, No-2

Is there any opportunity for voluntary savings?

Yes-1, No-2
If yes, amount of voluntary savings:__________
If no, any specific reason:____________

6.11 Frequency of savings:
Weekly-1, Bi-Weekly-2, Monthly-3, Bi-monthly-4, More than that (specify)

6.12 From where do you find money to deposit for savings?
From own income-1, From family members' income-2,

6.13 Do you know whether savings money is collected regularly from all members?

Yes-1, No-2
If yes, how did you know it?
It is announced at the end of the meeting-1, I ask the other members-2,

Others tell me-3, any other (specify)-4: ___________

6.14 Is the SHG linked to any bank/NGO/MFI?

Yes-1, No-2

If yes, name: ______________________

6.15 How many months after the formation of the SHG is credit linked with the bank/NGO/MFI? After________ months

6.16 Are you satisfied with the workings of your supporting institution like bank/NGO/government agency?

Yes-1, No-2

If no, reason ______________________

6.17 Any training programmes organised by your supporting institution?

Yes-1, No-2

If yes, programmes conducted in last year:

Type of programme	Number of times	How many of your SHG members attended
Training		
Demonstration		
Study tour		

How the member are selected for above programmes:_______________

7. SHG operational indicators:

7.1 Do you have freedom of participation in SHG affairs?

Yes-1, No-2,

If yes, very actively-1, actively-2, seldom-3, never-4

If no, reason:_______

7.2 Transparency in SHG activities:

Always-1, Sometimes-2, Rarely-3, Never-4

7.3 Trust in other member:

Very good-1, Always-2, Sometime-3 ,Very bad-4, Never-5

7.4 Communication with members:

Very good-1, Always-2, Sometime-3 ,Very bad-4, Never-5

7.5 Risk involved:

Least risk-1, Less risk-2, Some risk-3, More risk-4, Most risk-5

7.6 How do you select officers of your SHG?

Through election-1, through consensus-2

7.7 Do all members have equal opportunity to become office bearer?

Yes- 1, No-2

7.8 Are there any subgroups within SHG?

Yes-1, No-1

If yes, reason:______________

7.9 Are there any conflicts among members in SHG?

Yes-1, No-1

If yes, how are they solved?

____

7.10 How are the decisions taken in the SHG?

Arrive at a consensus after discussing the matter in the SHG-1,

Decided by majority after discussing the matter in the SHG-2,

Leaders and committee members-3, As per norms from authority-4,

Any other (specify):____________

7.11 Group Cohesion rating:

Below average-1, Average-2, Above average-3, Outstanding-4

8. SHG loan disbursement indicators:

8.1 Who selects the beneficiary for loans?
NGO-1, Government official-2, Bank-3, Committee members-4,
The whole group in meeting-5

8.2 Are there are any informal rules that play a role in overriding the loan sanction?
Yes-1, No-2
If yes, specify:___________________

____

8.3 Do you need to give any loan-sanctioning incentives to any body within or outside SHG?
Yes-1, No-2
If yes, specify:_______________

____

8.4 Who decides the interest rate for loans?
NGO-1, Government official-2, Bank-3, Committee members-4,
The whole group in meeting-5

8.5 What steps does SHG take for delay in payment of loan by members?
Extend the period without fine-1, Extend the period with fine-2,
Any other (specify)-3, __________________

8.6 If somebody defaults on loans repayment, who decides the fine or punishment?
NGO-1, Government official-2, Bank-3, Committee members-4,
The whole group in meeting-5, not applicable-6

9. **Members' economic information:**

9.1 Do you have any other financial savings?
Chits-1, Private savings-2, Informal deposits-3, Insurance-4,
Any other-5 (specify) ___________, No-6

9.2 What was the source of finance in your contingency before joining the SHG?
1.
2.
3.

9.3 Had your family taken loans from moneylenders or other informal sources before joining SHG?
Yes-1, No-2, Don't know-3

9.4 Taking loan from moneylenders or informal sources after joining the SHG:
Increased-1, Decreased-2, No change-3
If increased or no change,
Reasons:
Don't get sufficient loans from SHGs-1, Haven't repaid the loans from SHG yet-2, Delay in getting the loans from SHG-3, Any other (specify)-4, N/A-5

9.5 Have taken loans from this source after joining the SHG?
Yes-1, No-2

If yes, give details

Purpose of loan	Total amount (Rs.)	No. of times	Interest rate	Repayment status
Consumption				
IGA				
Other loans				

Consumption loan: Food-1, Clothing-2, Education-3, Marriage-4, Festival needs-5, Other (specify)-6

Income-generation activity loans (IGA): Agriculture-1, Animal husbandry-2, Petty business-3, Any other (specify)-4

Other loans: Purchasing of land-1, Construction/maintenance of well-2, Construction/maintenance of house-3, Repayment of old loans-4, Reclaiming mortgage loan-5, any other (specify)-6

Repayment status: Fully paid-1, Regularly paying-2, Paying irregularly-3, Not yet started-4

9.6 Is there any subsidy provided for the loan sanctioned?

Yes-1, No-2

If yes, who will provide?____________

And how much:_____________

9.7 Mode of repayment:

I. Number of instalments:__________________

II. Amount/instalment: ___________________

III. Available duration for repayment :_____________________

IV. Instalment stipulation is convenient for SHG and for its members:

Yes-1, No-2

If no, reasons: _________, ___________________,________________

9.8 Have you ever been a defaulter before?
Yes-1, No-2
If yes, reason for becoming defaulter:

____

What measure is taken by SHG against you for becoming defaulter?
1.
2.
3.

9.9 Have you taken bank loan with the help of SHG for IGA?
Yes-1, No-2

10. SHG and social issues:

10.1 How often do you discuss social problems/issues in SHG meetings?
Very often-1, Sometimes-2, Never-3
If yes, what issues?
1.
2.
3.

10.2 Are there any activities/programmes taken by your SHG in resolving social issues or community problems?
Yes-1, No-2
If no, reason:
Fear of isolation-1, Focus only on savings and loan-2, Lack of cooperation for such issues-3, Lack of time-4 , N/A-5

If yes, explain:

Any change occurred? Positive-1, Negative-2, No change-3

10.3 Is there any political influence/control in functioning of SHG by any means?
Yes-1, No-2
If yes, how do they control/influence?

____

____

11. **(For those who have taken up income-generating activities)**

1. **Self-employment/Income generation (individual)**

1.1 Activity of the enterprise:____________

1.2 When was it started? __________

1.3 Have you got any training?

Yes-1 No-2 N/A-3

1.4 The total project cost in Rs:________

1.5 Loan amount: Rs_______ ; subsidy/ grant amount: Rs____

1.6 Beneficiary share amount: Rs ______

1.7 What type of loans?

Direct bank loans-1 NGO loans -2

Only from thrift-3 Any other (specify)-4

1.8 Average monthly profit:_______________

If no profit, why? _______________

1.9 Rough monthly expenses in Rs: __________

1.10 Status of repayment:

Fully paid-1, Regularly paying-2, Paying irregularly-3,
Not yet started-4, Defaulter-5

2. **Self-employment/Income generation (group)**

2.1 Activity of the enterprise:__________________

2.2 When was it started? __________

2.3 Have you got any training?
Yes-1 , No-2, N/A-0

2.4 Number of people engaged:____

2.5 Total project cost in Rs:________

2.6 Loans amount Rs:_______; Subsidy/grant amount Rs:____

2.7 Beneficial contribution amount Rs:_____

2.8 Is there any difficulty in getting beneficial contributions?

Yes-1, No-2

If yes, what is the difficulty? Please explain:

____

2.9 What type of loans?

Direct bank loans-1, NGO -2,

Only from thrift-3, Any other (specify)-4

2.10 Average monthly profit from this enterprise:______________

If no profit, why? ________________________________

2.11 Average monthly expenses in Rs:____________

2.12 Status of repayment:
Fully paid-1, Regularly paying-2, Paying irregularly-3,
Not yet started-4, Defaulter-5 ☐

12. Opinion:

13. Comments of the investigator:

Record ranking	Ranking Details
Marginal	A few basic records exist and are being maintained
Below average	All basic records exist, but only a few are maintained. Quality of minutes book is poor, containing only details of meeting date, number of members, financial transactions, and signatures.
Average	All basic records exist and are maintained, but are not up to date. Quality of minutes book is average, with details of meeting date, number of members, financial transactions, and discussions related to loan sanctions, monitoring, and default, along with signatures.
Above average	All basic records exist and are maintained and up to date, but not updated regularly each month. Quality of minutes book is average, with details of meeting date, number of members, financial transactions, discussions related to loan sanctions, monitoring, default, federation functioning (if any), and social aspects, along with signatures.
Complete and up to date	All basic records exist and are maintained and up to date, but contain errors and do not tally with financial statements.
Virtually no errors	All basic records exist and are maintained and up to date and have virtually no errors.

Overall rating of group functioning	Ranking criteria
Exceptional	Group meetings and savings and loan plus interest repayments are regular. Group norms exist and those related to attendance and savings are implemented. SHG has accessed loan from bank or federation.
Above average	Group meetings and savings and interest repayments are regular. Group norms exist, and those related to attendance and savings are implemented. SHG has accessed loan from bank or federation.
Average	Group meetings and savings are regular. Group norms exist but some or all are not implemented.
Below average	Group meetings are regular but not scheduled. Savings are regular, but group norms are not articulated.
Poor	Group exists but does not meet regularly. Savings and loan repayments are highly irregular.

Group Cohesion Rating (Collective functioning)	Ranking criteria
Below average	SHG decisions are made by leaders; all, except 1–2 members, attend meetings regularly and are aware of group transactions. Group meetings and savings are regular. Group norms exist but some or all are not implemented.
Average	SHG decisions are made by one leader; more than half of members attend meetings regularly and are aware of group transactions. Group meetings are regular but not scheduled. Savings are regular, but group norms are not articulated.
Above average	SHG decisions are made by leaders and 2–3 members; all, except 1–2 members, attend meetings regularly and participate in discussions. Group meetings and savings and interest repayments are regular. Group norms exist, and those related to attendance and savings are implemented. SHG has accessed loan from bank or federation.
Outstanding	The SHG makes decisions by consensus; all members attend meetings regularly and participate in discussions and decision-making. Group meetings and savings and loan plus interest repayments are regular. Group norms exist and those related to attendance and savings are implemented. SHG has accessed loan from bank or federation.

Annexure 10. Questionnaire for SHGs

The Performance of Microcredit Organisations – A Comparative Perspective

Date:

1. Name of the SHG:
2. Address:
3. Year of establishment of SHG:
4. **Sponsored by: Banks-1, Govt. agency -2, NGO-3** ☐
5. Nature of membership: Women only-1, Men only -2, Both-3 ☐
6. Age composition of members:

Age (years)	Number of members
18–25	
26–35	
36–45	
46–55	
56–65	
More than 65 years	

7. Education:

Level of education	Number of members
Illiterate	
Primary only	
Up to SSLC	
PUC	
Degree holders	
Diploma	
P.G. degree	

8. Religion:

Religion	Number of members
Hindu	
Muslim	
Christian	
Jain	
Other	

9. Caste :

Caste	Number of members
Brahmin	
Gowda	
Lingayath	
Kuruba	
SC/ST	
OBC	

10. Occupation of the members:

Occupation	Number of members
Agriculture	
Agri-labour	
Non agri-labourer	
Govt./Private service	
Small business	
housewife	
Craftsman (specify)	
Other (specify)	

11. Marital status:

Marital status	Number of members
Married	
Unmarried	
Widows	
Divorced	

12. Income status of SHG members:

Income range (per annum)	Number of members
Rs.5,000–10,000	
Rs.11,000–20,000	
Rs.21,000–30,000	
Rs.31,000–40,000	
Rs.41,000–50,000	
Rs.51,000–60,000	
Rs.61,000–70,000	

Rs.71,000–80,000	
Rs.81,000–90,000	
Rs.91,000–1,000,000	
Above Rs.1,000,000	

13. Organisational information on SHGs:

13.1 Is the SHG housed in separate premises? ☐
i. Yes-1, No-2

13.2 If yes: Owned- 1, Hired -2 ☐

13.3 Objectives of SHG:

i.

ii.

iii.

iv.

13.4 How do you select officers of your SHG? ☐
Through election-1, Through consensus-2

13.5 What is the term of office bearer? ☐
One year -1, Two years-2, More than 2 years (specify)-3

13.6 Do all members have equal opportunity to become office bearer? ☐
Yes- 1, No-2

13.7 Frequency of meetings to discuss the SHG affairs: ☐
Weekly-1, Bi-weekly-2, Monthly-3, Bi-monthly-4, More than that (specify)

13.8 Do all the members attend the meetings regularly? ☐
Yes-1, No-2

If no, reason:__________________

13.9 Attending meetings is.. ☐
Voluntary-1, Compulsory -2
Percentage of attendance:__________

13.10 Is there any action taken against the member who is not involving in any of the SHG activities? ☐
Yes-1, No-2
If yes:______________________________
If no: why?__________________________

13.11 **Details of membership:**

Details	
Total number of members at the time of establishment	
Members at present	
Dropouts	

I. Reasons for dropping out:

i.

ii.

iii.

II. Any prescribed membership fee for the members? ☐

Yes-1, No-2

If yes:

a) Initial membership fees?________________________

b) How do you use membership fees collected?_____________________

III. Do all who approach SHG get SHG membership? ☐

Yes-1, No-2

If no, are there any criteria to select?

1.

2.

3.

IV. Who will take decisions on selecting or giving SHG membership? ☐

All existing members-1, Office bearers-2,

Other-3 (specify)________

V. Frequency of savings:

Weekly-1, Bi-weekly-2, Monthly-3, Bi-monthly-4, More than that (specify) ☐

Savings amount per time:___________

Is there any opportunity for voluntary savings?

If yes, how many members have done it?

Amount (range)	Number of members

14. Group Cohesion Rating:

Below average-1, Average-2, Above average-3, Outstanding-4

15. Overall rating of group functioning:

Exceptional-1, Above average-2, Average-3, Below average-4, Poor-5

16. Record keeping:

Marginal-1, Below average-2, Average-3, Above average-4, Complete and up to date-5, Virtually no errors-6

Records maintained	Checklist
Attendance register	
Minutes book	
Savings ledger	
Cash book	
General ledger	
Bank pass book	
Receipts voucher file	
Payments voucher file	

17. Risk involved in SHG compared to other financial means:

Least risk-1, Less risk-2, Some risk-3, More risk-4, Most risk-5

18. Cost involved in acquiring the credit (transaction cost):

Least expensive-1, Less expensive-2, Quite expensive-3, Most expensive-4

19. **Capital resources of SHG:**

Capital resource	Amount (RS.)		
	2005–06	2006–07	2007–08
Membership fee			
Support from NGO/government/bank (NABARD)			
Savings of members deposited in bank			
Interest on deposits			
Interest from lending			

20. **Loans obtained from the bank/NGO/MFI by SHG**

Year	Purpose	Rate of interest	Amount (Rs.)	Repayment status

2005–06				
2006–07				
2007–08				

1. Do any informal rules play a role in overriding the loan sanction?
   Yes 1, No-2
   If yes, specify:__________________
   ____

2. Is there any subsidy provided for the loan sanctioned ?
   Yes-1, No-2

   If yes, who will provide?_____________

   And how much (amount)?_____________

3. Mode of repayment:
   V. Number of instalments:__________________
   VI. Amount/instalment: ____________________
   VII. Available duration for repayment:______________________
   VIII. Instalment stipulation is convenient for SHG and for its members:
   Yes-1, No-2
   If no, reasons: _________, ____________________,_________________

4. Who decides the interest rate for loans?
   NGO-1, Government official-2, Bank-3, Committee members-4,
   The whole group in meeting-5, others-6 (specify):__________

21. Has your SHG utilised the bank/NGO/MFI loan fully?

year	Bank/NGO/MFI loan eligibility amount over per cent of SHG deposits	Per cent of unutilised loan
2005–06		
2006–07		
2007–08		

If loans are unutilised, what were the reasons?
1.
2.

22. Loans given to members by SHG

Year	Rate of interest	Total amount (Rs.)	Repayment Status	Number of defaulters
2005–06				
2006–07				
2007–08				

23. Purpose of loan given to members by SHG

Purpose	Amount (Rs.)	Repayment status

1. Mode of repayment:

   Number of instalments:____________________

   Amount/instalment: ____________________

   Available duration for repayment: ____________________

   Instalment stipulation is convenient for SHG and for its members:

   Yes-1, No-2

   If no, reasons: __________, ____________________, ____________________

2. What steps does SHG take for delay in repayment of loan by members?

   Extend the period without fine-1, Extend the period with fine-2,
   Any other (specify)-3,________________

3. 2. If somebody defaults in loans repayment, who decides the fine or punishment?

   NGO-1, Government official-2, Bank-3, Committee members-4,
   The whole group in meeting-5, not applicable-6

4. What steps will be taken against defaulters?

24. Does the SHG have its own business activity?

Yes-1, No-2

If yes, give details:

____________________, ______________, ______________

25. Has the SHG used bank loan/NGO/MFI for its own activities?

Yes-1, No-2

If yes, details:

Purpose	Loan amount (Rs.)

26. SHG and social issues:

26.1 How often do you discuss the social problems/issues in SHG meetings?

Very often-1, Sometimes-2, Never-3

If yes, on which issues:

1.

2.

3.

26.2 Any of the activities/programmes taken by your SHG about resolving social issues or community problems?

Yes-1, No-2

If no, reason:

Fear of isolation-1, Focus only on savings and loan-2, Lack of cooperation for such issues-3, Lack of time-4 ,N/A-5

If yes, explain:

Any change occurred? Positive-1, Negative-2, No change-3

26.3 Is there any political influence/control in functioning of SHG by any means?

Yes-1, No-2

If yes, how are they controlling/influencing?

i. ____________________________

ii. ____________________________

27. What are the problems encountered by your SHG and did you overcome them?

1.

2.

3.

4.

28. What are the reasons for problems:

1.

2.

3.

4.

Your opinion:

***ibidem*-Verlag**
Melchiorstr. 15
D-70439 Stuttgart
info@ibidem-verlag.de

www.ibidem-verlag.de
www.ibidem.eu
www.edition-noema.de
www.autorenbetreuung.de

Zeitfracht Medien GmbH
Ferdinand-Jühlke-Straße 7
99095 Erfurt, Deutschland
produktsicherheit@kolibri360.de